TRANSITION

Transition *was founded in 1961 in*
Uganda by the late Rajat Neogy and quickly
established itself as a leading forum for
intellectual debate. The first series of issues
developed a reputation for tough-minded, far-
reaching criticism, both cultural and political,
and this series carries on the tradition.

CONTENTS

Cover Image: Photo courtesy of Thomas Sayers Ellis. Modified design by Zi Lin. © 2009 *Transition*

ONE OF THE paradoxes of the present situation in Africa, marked as it is by human disasters on a colossal scale and on a continual basis, has been the remarkable resurgence of the expressive arts all over the continent. Where one might have expected a thwarting of the creative spirit, a decline of productive capacities, and even a paralysis of will, we have witnessed instead sustained innovation at every level of cultural expression. This paradox is perhaps most evident in the case of the Democratic Republic of the Congo (DRC), where, amidst the harsh reality of a seemingly unending crisis and the large-scale suffering it has occasioned for its populations, the musicians have kept alive the appealing force of their art by constantly renewing their repertoire, integrating styles from other parts of the continent and beyond to produce some of the most joyful music in the world. In the process, *soukouss,* the musical form we associate with the DRC, has been undergoing transformation with the infusion of musical trends and performance styles derived from *zouk, reggae, makossa, afro-jazz,* and, more recently, *hip-hop.*

The same creative impulse, set against powerful odds, can be observed in other parts of the continent. Thus, for example, the depressing effect of the discourse around HIV/AIDS has not prevented the emergence of an original orientation of the arts in post-apartheid South Africa, one in which the violence of everyday life has been foregrounded as the focus of artistic reflection, as in the film *Tsotsi* (2005). And it is in the midst of severe economic deprivation and the moral disillusionment induced by a barely functioning state that Nigeria's "Nollywood" has burgeoned, its technical reinvention of the cinema testifying to a remarkable resourcefulness on the part of the producers, one which has, moreover, enabled a serious exploration of the social dilemmas that have plagued the country and the psychic tensions they have generated, as is evident in the new films devoted to the condition of women in Hausa society. It is pertinent that the renewal of the African novel, with its emphasis on the pressures created by the new urban situation in Africa, has been largely the work of female writers. The same creative energy is evident in other areas, such as painting, sculpture, and architecture. And it is surely a testimony to the awakening of the reflective spirit in Africa that, after decades of steady decline, publishing has acquired a new pace and momentum, with books originated on the continent serving more and more to fulfill the educational, intellectual, and cultural needs of the African people.

These trends serve as pointers to an awakening of consciousness in Africa, even as the continent continues to feature as the theater of a historic adversity created by forces within and without. They suggest new directions of thought and imagination that we at *Transition* intend to explore in all the areas in which they are becoming manifest. In upcoming issues, we will be looking ahead, with a view to discerning the movement of forces that are shaping African lives, their imprint on minds, and their consequences for the continent and its diaspora, at a time when a momentous turn of events has called attention to their common entanglement in the American experience.

—The Editors

UNIVERSITY OF
CALIFORNIA PRESS
JOURNALS + DIGITAL PUBLISHING

Sociology

CONTEXTS

EDITORS // Christopher Uggen and Douglas Hartman

An award-winning quarterly magazine of the American
Sociological Association, *Contexts* presents cutting-edge
perspectives on the most provocative issues facing contemporary society. This pioneering journal brings accessible, incisive writing and the best of sociological inquiry to
bear on crucial concerns such as poverty, education, pop
culture, immigration, religion, environmental justice, and
much more.

WWW.UCPRESSJOURNALS.COM

Individual, Community, and Human Rights

a lesson from Kwasi Wiredu's philosophy of personhood

Souleymane Bachir Diagne

ON AUGUST 12, 2008, at a time when the world was still dumbfounded by the sumptuous opening ceremony of the Beijing Olympic Games—as it would soon be by the "epics" of Michael Phelps and Usain Bolt—the well-known conservative columnist David Brooks published in the *New York Times* "Harmony and the Dream," a series of philosophical-political reflections inspired by the celebration of China's rise to the status of global superpower. At the center of these reflections lies the question of human rights. Interestingly, Brooks reads that question as another aspect of a cosmic clash of civilizations, a dimension of the cultural divide between cultures that value the individual above the community and those according to which, supposedly, the totality is everything.

Brooks's column begins by adducing psychology tests conducted by Dr. Richard Nisbett, described in *The Geography of Thought: How Asians and Westerners Think Differently—and Why*, published in 2003. Nisbett, who ran the University of Michigan at Ann Arbor Culture and Cognition Program, reports on the differences he judged significant between the cognitive approaches of subjects from the United States and those from countries in the Far East. With his international team of researchers, among them Chinese, Korean, and Japanese scientists, he observes, for example, that when presented with a fish tank, Asians are more likely to see the wider context, while Americans focus instead on individual objects, say, the biggest fish in the tank. The major conclusion that the team of scientists drew from their research is that, in general, "South Asian thought" (whatever that means—it remains to be seen if there is a denotation for that phrase) has a tendency to be more holistic than "Western thought" (again: whatever that means), for it seeks to embrace the totality of the field, minimizing the use of logical categories that exclude the coexistence of multiple perspectives. The Chinese philosophy of Feng Shui, the art of arranging objects with respect to the cosmic correlations that weave them together, could find here, apparently, an illustration.

I question the way in which the results of this research in comparative cognitive psychology have been hijacked by Brooks to reinforce the notion of a profound, civilizational rupture between the West and the East, especially when it comes to human rights, which are truly and naturally the rights of the individual. Brooks moves from narrow, cognitive questions to a much bigger picture, an array of human civilizations from the most individualistic to the most collectivist:

> You can create a global continuum with the most individualistic societies—like the United States or Britain—on one end, and the most collectivist societies—like China and Japan—on the other.

What characterizes individualistic countries, then, is supposed to be that they "tend to put rights and privacy first," while collectivist societies "tend to value harmony and duty." The notion that individualism has a history connected with that of capitalism is evoked only to be then relegated to an essentialist vision according to which the West is a natural continuation of ancient Greece, which is said to have particularly and uniquely valued "individual heroism"—as if such a value were not widely shared in the epics, literatures, and praise poetries of all cultures. In short, the few individualistic societies on the planet are alleged to be such **Human rights, are truly and naturally the rights of the individual.** in virtue of a unique *telos* that sets them apart. The far more numerous societies naturally inclined to value the group offer, on the model of China, the path of the "harmonious collective," which can be, says Brooks, "as attractive as the ideal of the American Dream." That is why, he continues, the new Chinese power "isn't only an economic event. It is a cultural one." As a consequence, this "other" culture of development is going to create the conditions for a "new sort of global conversation" between civilizations which are both irreconcilable in their different identities and bound to find ways to live together in peace.

The reason why I have reproduced the argument of Brooks's column is that the Huntingtonian paradigm that it draws upon, no matter how decried it may be for its simplistic cultural determinism, still colors, under different guises, the ways in which we think of concepts such as human rights as both a stake in and a foundation of a global public square. Thus, the very notion of a dialogue of cultures as a way out of their "clash"—supposedly inscribed in the very nature of things—is yet another tribute to that paradigm. And I agree with Amartya Sen, when he explains in *Identity and Violence: The Illusion of Destiny* (2006) that the alternative between clash or dialogue is a pitfall, since both *clash* and *dialogue* share the same premise, which needs to be reassessed: cultural identity as destiny. That said, it must be emphasized that what makes the illusion of "identity as destiny" function is less what is written by intellectuals such as Brooks, who have assigned

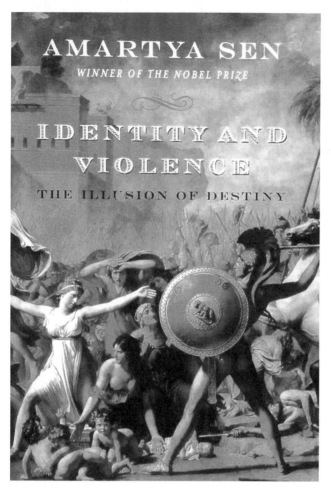

AMARTYA SEN
WINNER OF THE NOBEL PRIZE

IDENTITY AND
VIOLENCE
THE ILLUSION OF DESTINY

to themselves the task of celebrating the unique excellence of the *telos* of a "West" that naturally fathered democracy, public debate, individualism, and human rights, than it is the implicit acceptance of that representation by *other* intellectuals, who adopt, in principle, an anti-Western posture and undertake the symmetrical task of defending and illustrating *another* identity, which entails, for example, advocating *another* philosophy of human rights. Amartya Sen criticizes the "championing of 'Asian values'," which "flourished particularly in East Asia in the 1990s," as "anti-Western rhetoric" stemming from "an attitudinal climate that is obsessed with the West." The question becomes that of the possibility of the elements of a *postcolonial* world—both "de-Westernized" and "dis-Oriented," according to Emmanuel Levinas, because it has become a "saraband of innumerable cultures"—converging around a human universal that is presumed by a universal declaration of rights.

To take a concrete example, let us consider the African Charter on Human and Peoples' Rights. According to the Drafting Committee, it is designed to "reflect the African approach to human rights," that is, to model itself on the African philosophy of law and respond to the needs of Africa. Although the Charter was adopted in June 1981 by the eighteenth Conference of the Heads of States and Government of the Organization of African Unity (OAU) in Nairobi, it was only in 2006 that the Assembly of the Heads of States and Governments of the African Union (AU) activated the charter, by electing the eleven judges of the Commission in charge of its application.

It should be noted, first, that the Charter presents in one single document civil, political, economical, social, and cultural rights (that is also the case for the American Convention on Human Rights, adopted in 1969, which was obviously used as a model); second, that it insists particularly on peoples' rights, and what are designated as "the duties of the individual *vis-à-vis* the community," in order to reflect the unique importance of the *group* in African societies. Again, the opposition between individualistic and communitarian societies is considered a given by the drafters of the Charter, who in fact share Huntington and Brooks's world view according to which no enunciation of rights can actually bridge the gaps or umbrella the map, as it were, of our cultural differences. Now, does taking that supposed specificity into account imply, in practice, the necessity of adding collective rights to the internationally recognized ones? That seems to be the thinking here. But what should we make of a statement such as article 29, paragraph 7, which stipulates:

> the individual shall also have the duty . . . to preserve and strengthen positive African cultural values in his relations with other members of the society, in the spirit of tolerance, dialogue, and consultation, and, in general, to contribute to the promotion of the moral well-being of society.

This paragraph is immediately followed by an injunction "to contribute to the best of his abilities, at all times and at all levels, to the promotion and achievement of African unity." One can immediately see how wide open the doors of interpretation are: What are the *African cultural values*? When do they cease to be *positive*? And what does *positive* mean? One can guess the kind of complex issues that the drafters of the Charter had to deal with, being caught, as it were, between the will to affirm the primacy of the community in reflecting the "African philosophy of human rights," on the one hand, and the need to avoid seeing that same primacy trample the individual right to hold dissenting views and the freedom to express them, on the other. Hence the precision in noting that the values under consideration are the *positive* ones (and not, say, those entailing mutilations for the purpose of initiation) and that their preservation and reinforcement should be conducted "in the spirit of tolerance, dialogue, and consultation," which is to say: they should be promoted, not imposed.

The alternative between clash or dialogue is a pitfall, since both *clash* and *dialogue* share the same premise: cultural identity as destiny.

More generally, article 29 establishes a list of duties *vis-à-vis* the national community—and even the security of the State, which is then assumed, apparently, to represent *ipso facto* that community—that the individual is invited to fulfill by "by placing his physical and intellectual abilities at its service." Article 29 thus concentrates all the difficulties of weaving together the rights of the community, the rights of the individual, and the duties of the latter *vis-à-vis* the former.

It should be noted that Amnesty International, which has published a brochure of the text of the Charter to use as an instrument in its mission to prevent human rights abuses on the continent, has also commented that, of course, "the duty to contribute to the national defense in accordance with the law must be qualified by the right to freedom of conscience and religion." Such a precision is crucial because one can imagine a situation where it is decreed that what "the community" demands is to enlist "physical and intellectual abilities at the service" of a certain concept of the identity of the community and what it means to preserve it, thus criminalizing any dissidence. In fact, *What is the community?* is not a question that one can easily answer, and to make the community the bearer of human rights, and to define duties toward its preservation, predisposes one to an incarcerating conception of identity, one which eventually endangers the very notion of human rights.

What are the *African cultural values*? When do they cease to be *positive*? And what does *positive* mean?

• • •

THE QUESTION MUST be now posed: *Must an African philosophy of what it means to be human and, as such, to have rights be caught up in a communitarian approach?* The response is clear: *Absolutely not.* And, to be convinced of this, one needs only to consider perhaps the most important and ancient documents on human rights in Africa, namely, the so-called Oath of the Manden, proclaimed in the early thirteenth century—1222 is generally accepted—by the founder of the Mali empire, Sunjata Keita. The West African secret society of the Hunters has been the memory and the guardian of the Oath ever since. Let me quote from it three articles, beginning with the first:

> The Hunters declare: Every (human) life is a life. It is true that a life comes to existence before another life, but no life is more "ancient," more respectable than another life, just as no life is superior to another life.

The sixth article states:

> The Hunters declare: the root of slavery is extinct on this day, from a wall to the other, from a border of the Manden to the other; *razzia* is banned in the Manden from now on, the torments created by those horrors are over, starting this day in the Manden. What a trial torments are! Especially when the oppressed has no recourse. For the slave is given no consideration, nowhere in the world.

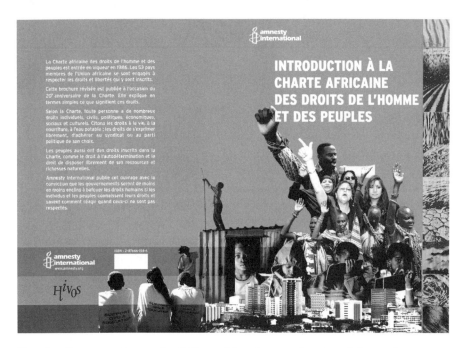

Finally, the seventh article, followed by the conclusion of the oath, states:

> People from ancient times tell us: "man as an individual made of bones and flesh, marrow and nerves, of skin covered with hackles and hair, is nourished by food and drinks; but his soul, his spirit lives out of three things: to see whom he wants to see, to say what he wants to say, and to do what he wants to do; should one of these things be missing for the human soul, it would certainly suffer from it and wilt."

Consequently, the Hunters declare:

> From now on everyone shall enjoy self-determination,
> Everyone shall be free in their actions,
> Everyone shall dispose of the fruits of their labor.
> This is the Oath of the Manden for the rest of the world
> to hear.

One immediate conclusion to draw from this text is that the notion of a declaration or an oath to promote the rights attached to human life is the prerogative of no particular civilization. Amartya Sen often cites, on that question, the pursuit by the Indian emperor Akbar of what he has called "the path of reason [*rahi aql*]," which led him to proclaim, among other articles, freedom of conscience in unequivocal terms: "No one should be interfered with on account of religion, and anyone is to be allowed to go over to a religion that pleases him."

Secondly, the vision of humanity manifested in the Hunters' oath has not encumbered itself with considerations of the value of the community and the duties of the individual toward it. The approach is straightforwardly individualistic, because every life is individual and unique. As we could put it, paraphrasing the first words of the Oath by emphasizing in the English rendition one particular word, *Every life is* one *life*.

I would like now to draw a practical conclusion and offer a few reflections on the importance for us today of the light shed by Kwasi Wiredu on the dialectic of individual/community. First, the text of the African Charter on Human and Peoples' rights is deeply flawed when it comes to its "communitarian" articles, as they are written in such a way that they end up almost codifying as human rights statements what could well express some *raison d'état* entirely contrary to individual rights. And, if that is the consequence of a philosophical misunderstanding of the dialectic between individual and community, then it should be the task of African philosophers to critically reflect, more than they have done so far, on a text that has been in general too neglected in our scholarship, even when dealing with the same questions of the relationship between personhood, individual, community, and rights. After all, the Charter is—or should be—an important tool for African integration and unity.

The notion of a declaration or an oath to promote the rights attached to human life is the prerogative of no particular civilization.

Kwasi Wiredu calls for a raised consciousness regarding the importance of such a task:

> How to devise a system of politics that, while being responsive to the developments of the modern world, will reflect the best traditional thinking about human rights . . . is one of the profoundest challenges facing modern Africa.

The distinction that Wiredu here establishes, between a descriptive conception of a *person* among the Akan people and a normative concept, is crucial. On the descriptive level, we are told, a person is the individual who received from God "life principle and destiny [*okra*]," who inherited from her mother a "lineage [*mogya*]," and who owes a certain "presence [*sunsum*]" to her father. But what truly defines *personhood* is what one has to be, his *to ti en einai*, as Aristotle would say. Therefore, Wiredu explains:

> personhood is not something you are born with, but something you may achieve, and it is subject to degrees, so that some are more *onipa* [persons] than others, depending on the degree of fulfillment of one's obligations to self, household, and community.

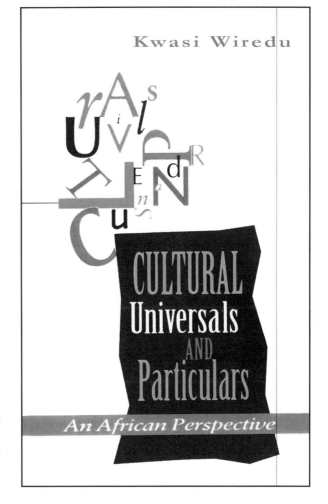

Kwasi Wiredu

CULTURAL
Universals
AND
Particulars
An African Perspective

What Wiredu says about *becoming-person* in Akan society shows, I think, the flaw identified above in the Charter's communitarian articles: ontological primacy of the community is the *raison d'être* of the individual's duties *vis-à-vis* the group, whereas we should understand those duties as a part of the individual's process of *becoming-person*. So, on the one hand, it is recognized that the human being is fully complete and can achieve his destiny only in the community, as a *social animal*, in Aristotelian terms—or as in an Akan adage cited by Wiredu, "when a human being descends upon the earth s/he lands in a town." On the other hand, the duty to become a person through the group and, in particular, through service to the group is affirmed and remains inscribed in the individual trajectory of a life seeking self-realization. As another Akan adage cited by Wiredu puts it, "nobody was there when I was taking my destiny from my God."

This seems to me a fundamental lesson that Wiredu's work on Akan philosophy teaches and on which we need to meditate in the task of critically elaborating a Charter of Human Rights by which Africa recognizes the universal and herself as a part of it. More generally, we need to create a global public square founded on public reasoning and our common humanity.

What is said about the Akan is very similar to what is said in other African cultures about the dialectic of the individual and the community—witness the very concept of *ubuntu* that Nelson Mandela has placed at the center of his thinking. And since I began with the Olympic Games, let me finish on a sportive note as well, by way of response to Brooks's cultural determinism. In addressing the challenge of building a team out of basketball stars who are individualistic to the point of selfishness, Boston Celtics coach Doc Rivers has adopted, with some success, the philosophy of *ubuntu* in teaching Kevin Garnett, Paul Peirce, Ray Allen, and their other teammates. Citing the proverb that summarizes it—*umuntu ngumuntu ngabantu* [a person is a person through other persons]—the coach asked his superstars to understand the truth that "I can't be all I can unless you are all you can be." Indeed.

The Myth of *Tribe* in African Politics

Ngũgĩ wa Thiong'o

I AM A literary humanist, and democratic ideals appeal to me. At the heart of the democratic or any political process in society is the question of power. In fact, we can define *politics* simply as the organization of power in society. Who or what social group holds power? For whom do they exercise that power? What are the ends toward which that power is exercised? The questions are valid for the system of laws and norms within nations, and also for the laws and norms that govern relations between nations, what goes by the name of *international relations*. Those same questions underlie the Lincolnian definition of *democracy* as the government of the people, by the people, for the people. In some ways, the most important elements in that definition are the three tiny connectives *of*, *by*, and *for*. For the Lincolnian definition to apply, the three connectives must be in place. Many governments and states fall short of the Lincolnian democratic ideal, because they leave out one or more of those connectives. Which connectives are emphasized, left out, or followed through, affects the ends for which power is exercised.

The values toward which power is exercised is a moral question. Laws are the instruments chosen by society for the proper control and exercise of power to ensure that they meet those ends embedded in their formulation. Law is a rule, a statement of *oughtness*, but, in contrast to other rules, law has a coercive component, the tools that ensure compliance. The *thou shalt not kill* of the biblical ten commandments is different from the *you must not kill* of the largely secular jurisprudence, because the latter spells out clearly the enforceable consequences of its infringement. The statement of a rule, its application, and the coercive component raise moral issues involving, for instance, the congruence of law—or lack thereof—with justice, and the moral limits of the use of the coercive component of law, such as issues of using torture to extract information from a citizen. So, no matter what angle we take, the questions of power in society, even within a democratic framework, come back to those of morality.

• • •

NOT SURPRISINGLY, THE words through which a certain law is formulated are the subject of debates about the use and interpretation of words. The exercise of democratic ideals—or the statement of law and its application—within and between nations is often conditioned by both our self-perception and our perception of the *other*. Self-perception and the perception of the other are often conditioned by definitions of words. For instance, democracy in ancient Athens was actually direct democracy, where every citizen of the *polis* was able to cast his vote on matters of war and peace. Direct democracy, as opposed to representative democracy, is an excellent ideal. But, then, the same democracy was predicated on the alleged fact that women, slaves, and foreigners—*barbarians*, as they were called—were not citizens. The word *citizen* determines inclusion or exclusion. The American Declaration of Independence talked glowingly in almost *Social Contract*–like Rousseauian terms about the fact that people were created equal and endowed by their creator with certain inalienable rights, but then excluded blacks and women from the category of *people*. In war, certain word usages can dehumanize the other—*Commies, Viet Congs*, etc.—and hence remove any moral scruples in dealing with them. Words become very important in the power relations between individuals and groups, in the exercise of law and democratic ideals. They help define the *other*: a member of a group with *other* religious, racial, gender, or biological affiliations.

A good example is the use of the five-letter English word *tribe*. The Western media's analysis of events in Africa reveals the word as the main obstacle in the way of a meaningful illumination of dynamics in modern Africa. *Tribe*— with its clearly pejorative connotation of the primitive and the premodern—is contrasted with *nation*, which connotes a more positive sense of arrival at the modern. Every African community is a *tribe*, and every African a *tribesman*. We can see the absurdity of the current usages, where thirty million Yorubas are referred to as a *tribe*, but four million Danes as a *nation*. A group of 250,000 Icelanders constitutes a nation, while 10 million Ibos make up a tribe. And yet, what's commonly described as a *tribe*, when looked at through objective lenses, fulfills all the criteria of shared history, geography, economic life, language, and culture that are used to define a *nation*. These critical attributes are clearly social and historical, not biological.

Thirty million Yorubas are referred to as a tribe, but four million Danes as a *nation*.

Nonetheless, to the analysts, *tribe* is like a genetic stamp on every African character, explaining his every utterance and action, particularly *vis-à-vis* other African communities. Using the same template of *Tribe X* versus *Tribe Y*, print and electronic media and even progressive thinkers simply look at the ethnic origins of the leading actors in a conflict and immediately place them in the category of X or Y. So, whatever the crisis, in whatever part of Africa, in whatever time period, the analysts arrive at one explanation: it is all because of the traditional enmity between Tribe X and Tribe Y. It is like looking at John McCain, seeing that he was born in Panama; then looking at Barack Obama, seeing that he was born in Hawaii; and then concluding that their political differences are due to the places of their birth or that their differences are rooted in an assumed traditional enmity between Panamanians and Hawaiians.

This template of *Tribe X* versus *Tribe Y* dominated discussions of the 2007 political crisis in Kenya, framing it in terms of the Luo and the Gikuyu, simply because Raila Odinga, then the opposition leader, now Prime Minister, was Luo, and Mwai Kibaki, the president, was Gikuyu. What did not fit into that neat composition was often glossed over. For instance, Gikuyu and the Luo people never shared boundaries, so the claim that they could have been traditional enemies defeats reason and common sense, but analysts were undaunted in their persistent use of the formula. Even the fact that the two leaders had followers across other communities, or the fact that much of the gruesome anti-Gikuyu ethnic cleansing came largely from Eldoret North, a Kalenjin area, and Narok, an area under Maasai dominance, was ignored, in order not to muddy the waters of the familiar formula of *Tribe X* versus *Tribe Y*.

Many newspapers talked of a continuous Gikuyu dominance in economics and politics throughout the entire forty-five years of Independence, and even before. The British ruled Kenya as a white settler state for sixty years, from about 1895 to 1963. Kenyatta, a Gikuyu, ruled for fifteen years, from 1963 to 1978. Moi, a Kalenjin, not a Gikuyu, ruled for the next twenty-four, from 1978 to 2002. Yet the discussions on events unfolding in Kenya rarely mentioned the sixty years of British settler rule or the twenty-four years of Moi dictatorship. The media and experts on Kenya developed a strange amnesia, yanking twenty-four years of Moi dictatorship off the pages of Kenyan postcolonial history, the better to have a narrative of Luo versus Gikuyu, or one of an uninterrupted Gikuyu dominance and privilege.

This does not mean that different African communities—whether now or earlier—have not harbored animosity toward each other. In fact, it is true that in precolonial Africa various communities fought over disputed property and territory and engaged in wars of conquest and domination. The vaunted empires of Ghana, Mali, Zulu, and Ashanti were built on conquest and maintained through systems of subjugation and tutelage. But there were also long periods when those same groups' relationships with others were characterized by peace and commerce. In this, there is nothing peculiarly African. All relationships between communities in history have alternated between hostility and hospitality. Whatever else may have been the case, these communities did not see themselves as living for the sole purpose of waging war.

Anaheet Gazder, *Native Roots*. 2008. Ink on paper, 8.5 × 11 inches

• • •

IT IS FAIR to say that *tribe*, *tribalism*, and *tribal wars*, the terms so often used to explain conflict in Africa, were colonial inventions. Most African languages do not have the equivalent of the English word *tribe*, with its pejorative connotations that sprung up in the evolution of the anthropological vocabulary of eighteenth- and nineteenth-century European adventurism in Africa. The words have companionship with other colonial conceptions, such as *primitive*, the *Dark Continent*, *backward races*, and *warrior communities*.

In slave and colonial conquests, Europeans would ally with one African community to subjugate another, not in the interest of the African ally, but in their own imperial interests. Where before there were rules governing warfare between communities—protection of women and children, for instance—now massacres of those who resisted were encouraged. There is no colonial story anywhere which does not contain grim episodes of wanton massacres of men, women, and children. Historian David Stannard certainly documents incidents of genocidal practices against native peoples in his 1992 book *American Holocaust*. Such genocidal practices are preceded by demonization and dehumanization through words. Sometimes, the ally who helped to subjugate the neighboring communities was later turned into a conquered subject, made to live in the same territory with the communities they had helped to conquer. Colonial states deliberately kept the colonized peoples in perpetual tension through the well-known imperial tradition of *divide and rule*.

Tribe, tribalism, and tribal wars, the terms so often used to explain conflict in Africa, were colonial inventions.

Often, the colonial state would use one community as the source of the army, another as the source of the police, and yet another as the source of labor, while others were kept as "tribal" specimens of the primitive, a living museum of the true "cultural" African, with his spear and animal skin. From all the communities would also come a small pool of intellectual labor: Africans educated in the colonial government and missionary schools became junior cadres of the colonial administration and Christian enterprise. Over time, the cumulative effects of these policies and practices stoked and deepened bitterness not toward the colonial state but often toward one another, with the colonizer presenting himself as the arbiter between the "eternally" hostile communities. A rationale often used to defend colonialism was that the imperial conquerors had stopped "tribal" wars.

• • •

The clash between Africa and Europe in the colonizing process was essentially one between the advanced capitalism of the time and precapitalist peasant economies. A hallmark of capitalism in general, but especially in colonial capitalism, is uneven regional development. With extraction of minerals and the development of monocrop economies—thus turning arable land from food production to the cultivation of coffee, tea, sisal, and cocoa as raw materials for export—the colonial economy served and complemented that of the mother country. While the colony as a whole served the mother country with raw materials, the rural areas within it served the towns with labor and food supply. Towns and cities were, of course, the hubs of capitalist activity. The regions around them gained from improved infrastructures and access to market and other facilities, however limited the access and the returns.

Colonial states deliberately kept the colonized peoples in perpetual tension through the well-known imperial tradition of *divide and rule*.

But capitalist enterprise also deepened uneven social development, especially in those regions that were the sources of labor. An underpaid working class, often divorced from the soil, emerged from those communities. Also emerging was a middle-class that gained from the fallouts of capitalist enterprise and colonial administration. So, to the problem of uneven regional development was added that of uneven social development within each region.

Since regions coincided with linguistic communities, uneven regional and social development affected the communities differently. Naturally, this deepened divisions within and between communities. Anticolonial resistance movements always tried to bridge the gaps within and between these communities. A social vision of a different future of freedom, democracy, and economic welfare helped to forge a national consciousness.

But the colonial state was always on the lookout against any positive rapprochements between communities. In Kenya, for instance, the British settler state would not allow the formation of a nationwide social or political organization among Africans. European settlers, and even Asian immigrants, could organize nationally, but Africans were allowed to organize labor, social, and political unions only within ethnic boundaries. The divisive tactics of the colonial regime reached their peak during the Mau Mau–armed struggle from 1952 to 1960, when Africans could form parties only along district lines. It was not until 1960, barely three years before independence, that the colonial state permitted countrywide political parties.

Taken as a whole, these measures and practices encouraged ethnic consciousness; the "biological system" they came to call "tribalism" derived, of course, from the conception of the *tribe* as a monolithic genetic entity. The history and usage of this one English word, *tribe*, have had negative effects on the evaluation and self-evaluation of Africa, for African intellectuals have internalized this divisive inheritance of colonialism. They have come to see each other through the colonial invention of the tribe, tribalism, and tribal wars, elevating cultural marks of difference such as distinct rituals, and even languages, as the real basis of divisions and communal identity. The subtext is clear: leave all reason at the door before you enter the chamber of African conflicts.

To explain problems in terms of the biological makeup of the characters is to express social despair, for if a problem has biological roots, its solution can only be biological. All of this has coalesced into indifference to African lives by the international and national middle classes. This attitude may explain, in part, why people—including Africans—can watch genocide in Rwanda and Darfur and not feel the urgency to act, as if they were waiting for biology to sort itself out. Political dictatorships—some even sponsored by the West—emerge, and people shrug their shoulders, eliciting the unspoken or spoken view: *Tribal mentality, so difficult to penetrate*. As for the African middle class, self-hatred from years of internalizing the colonial gaze makes some among them gleeful at the humiliation of another African. Political mismanagement as a negation of democratic and social rights is altogether ignored, and ethnic cleansing, the negation of the basic human right to life, is tolerated. But African problems, like those of any other peoples in history, have economic, political, and social roots. They arise historically, not biologically.

The subtext is clear: leave all reason at the door before you enter the chamber of African conflicts.

• • •

MANY YEARS AGO, I wrote that there are only two tribes in Africa, the *Haves* and the *Have-nots*, and these are to be found in all communities in varying degrees of intensity. But the *Haves* of one community tend to point to the *Haves* of another community as the only *Haves*, or else label an entire community as the *Have-it-Alls*. Political warlords, often millionaires themselves, then emerge as the defenders of the community against the enemy community of *Haves*. This allows political warlords to talk about ethnic purity as the key to economic and political liberation. These warlords often make sweetheart deals with Western companies—or are promised such deals, should they ever come to power. The Congo provides the best example: even in the so-called "tribal" wars—meaning among the political warlords—there is always the outsider who wants to see what he can pick from the ruins. So I should note the real existence of a third "tribe": the corporate tribe of the West.

In the case of Kenya, a look at the underlying problems, colonial legacies, uneven development, the deepening and widening gap between the rich and the poor, weak democratic institutions, the devastation of the national psyche by twenty years of a Western-backed Moi dictatorship, and the continuous dominance of Western interests would have ruined the neat narrative of Tribe X against Tribe Y. But it might have made us see that there were lessons the world could learn from the Kenyan crisis, for example, that a fair economic playground within and between nations is important for the exercise of democratic ideals. Seeing Africa in terms of nonrational mystical terms such as *tribe* and *tribalism* prevents people from seeing Africa's problems as a part of global concerns. And yet, the basic roots of instability in Africa are clearly the same as those that underlie a much broader instability today, in the era of globalization.

People shrug their shoulders, eliciting the unspoken or spoken view: *Tribal mentality, so difficult to penetrate.*

The world today is characterized by two rifts that deepen and widen daily. One is between the wealth of a group of largely Western nations and a majority of poor nations, primarily in Africa, Asia, and Latin America. As it is characterized by one of my characters in *Wizard of the Crow* (2006), this is the rift between the givers and recipients of charity, between credit/donor nations and beggar/debt-burdened nations. And yet, the natural resources of the debtor nations feed the creditor nations. The other rift is found within each and every nation in the world where a small social stratum stands on mass poverty below. Within these nations, the beggars and the homeless multiply; prisons harbor millions who could easily constitute a nation, were they living in a territory all their own. My contention is that these rifts between and within nations constitute the roots of great instability in the world today. Democratic ideals must come to terms with economic ideals for the empowerment of the least among us. What is needed is less mysticism and more rational analysis of social situations—whether in Africa or elsewhere. Progress and development need to be measured from the standpoint of those at the bottom of the mountain and not those at the top. Only then will reason, law, and democratic ideals be in accord with social justice.

This essay has been adapted from a lecture given by the author on April 28, 2008, as the holder of the 2008 Dan and Maggie Inouye Distinguished Chair in Democratic Ideals at the University of Hawaii at Manoa.

Five Poems from *Sonata Mulattica*

by Rita Dove

Hear Ye!

London, 1790

The Learned Pig, the Mechanical Turk, the Frenchman Tripping Over
the Plume in His Tricorner Hat—pass them by, the Season's begun!
You can't be seen slopping about the lower spectrum of open air
entertainment. Two shillings will buy you an hour of Musical Glasses
played by the delicious Miss Ford—no water in her cups,
yet they'll warble with no need of a drop! Speaking of which,

you look dry, Sir: a tuppence a tipple. Keep it moving,
that's the stuff; even if you've nowhere to get to—hurry on,
or you'll be trampled in the press. Choices! That's London:
You could follow the Janissary jingling through St. James
or stop in at Boodle's if your game is on. If you must join in,
amateur glees are sung every Friday at the Crown and Anchor,

with bawdy lyrics to follow when the ladies depart.
Feeling noble? Attend Sunday's benefit
for the castrato Tenducci, mired in debtor's prison;
Mondays are for war orphans, Tuesdays, syphilitics,
Wednesdays, for the Lying-In at Hospital in Westminster.
Got a watch? Guard the fob. Push on, past the rug beater, broom peddler,

the boy hawking pickles, the child twitching her broken tambourine.
Dodge clattering carts and trundling barrows, clacking spokes and doors
slamming on the four-in-hands heading over to Rotten Row for a highbrow
hobnob. Say what? Can't hear—what with fish hags haranguing
and unctuous urchins and flatulent hurdy-gurdies thumping out sea
    shanties
while rival churches toll the hours. You'd be better off examining

Charles Clagget's Ever-Tuned Organ at the King's Arms in Cornhill
or the Welsh harp at Whitehall. Failing a thirst for the exotic,
there's the orchestra at Vauxhall Gardens, oratorios at Covent Garden,
Salomon's subscription concerts in the rooms at Hanover Square.
Granted, nothing compares to the sight of Cotter the Giant
pulling a dwarf from his coat pocket (despite his size, Count Boruwlaski's

quite successful with the ladies); but if you're in the market for
condensed miracles, try the arias currently swelling Pantheon's rafters—
remarkable sonorities emanating from the tiny form of the inimitable
Madame Mara, guaranteed to snap the cords of your heart.
Smaller still? Ten-year-old Clement's always a good show, but for pure
flourish and spectacle, his rainbow opposite can be seen nightly

playing onstage at the Drury Lane Theatre: Little Mulatto Prince
George, fiddling away between Acts I and II of Handel's *Messiah*.

The Performer

Adagio sostenuto / Presto / Tempo primo

I step out.
I step out into silence.
I step out to take
my place; my place is silence
before I lift the bow and draw
a fingerwidth of ache upon the air.
This is what it is like

to be a flame: furious
but without weight, breeze
sharpening into wind, a bright gust
that will blind, flatten all of you—
yet tender,
somewhere inside
tender. If you could see me

now, Father, you would cry—though
you wept easily, as I remember,
and even so it was manly,
the way that thick black fist
daubed your cheek
with those extravagant sleeves
quivering.
                I prefer to stand,

cheek cushioned, and soothe her
as I pull the sobs out,
gently . . . yes, you hear it.
You who made me can hear it—
just as he's making me
hear it now, so that I can
pull it from her.

Andante con Variazioni

Thank you. It was a privilege. You are so kind.
It is all his doing; I am merely the instrument.
To have the honor of this premiere . . .
a beauty of a piece, indeed.

What an honor! Countess, I am enchanted.
I only wish I could better express my gratitude
in your lovely language: *Vielen Dank.*
It is all his—why, thank you, sir. I am speechless.

Gern geschehen, Madame; did I say that correctly?
(God I sound like my father.)
I believe he is pleased. I sincerely hope so . . .
but you are kindness incarnate. No, my privilege entirely.

Herr van Beethoven is indeed a Master, and Wien
an empress of a city. My apologies—
I only meant that she is . . . magnificent.
(Ludwig, get me out of here!)

Finale

If this world could stop
for a moment
and see me;
if I could step out
into the street and become
one of them,
one of anything,
I would sing—
no, weep right here—to simply
be and be and be . . .

Augarten, 7 AM

Spectator One

> Heavenly, to escape the city's poisons
> and breathe honey, honey, honey!
> All praise Morning's cathedral,
> the ranks of noble linden presiding:
> May we be privileged to pass through
> their green light and feathered fragrance
> with tipped hats and mute nods,
> Amen!

The British Ambassador

> . . . There goes Schuppanzigh, huffing up the aisle
> in his entrepreneurial trappings.
> Dear God, the man expands weekly!
> Ah, the Archduke. And Prince Lobkowitz,
> poor soul . . . such an unsightly specimen
> and feels just as miserable as he looks.
> I would have ended it years ago, gone out like a man.

Spectator Two

> Curious beginning—solo violin,
> reminiscent of Bach but wilder, a supplication—
> and the piano's reply is almost a lover's,
> a bird on a cliff returning its true mate's call.

Child

> He moves around too much.
> He's like a poplar in the wind!

Spectator Three

> For a savage he plays quite nicely.
> As for his figure—tall, slim,
> dare I say *elegant*? I'd heard
> he was a charmer, but never thought
> chimney soot applied to countenance
> could be considered handsome.

Spectator Two

What a furious storm he rides!
And Beethoven listing side to side
in accord with the gale,
bobbing that Rumpelstiltskin head
as if to say "Well done, my boy." . . .
That's it—a father to his prodigal son,
come home at last.

British Ambassador

To call this a sonata is obscene.
A Presto is presto and Adagio . . .
well, slow is meant to stay slow.
This Beethoven is as loopy as they say—
imagine, insulting the Prince
when he simply requested a song,
smashing figurines, dashing off
in the middle of dinner!

Spectator One

I thought that infernal back-and-forth
would never cease. A concert's meant
for reverie, to drift away
on nature's curative susurrations . . .
ah, a *Theme and Variations*—
that's more like it.

Child

I like his waistcoat.
How can he see out
from all that darkness?

Eroica

Beethoven at Castle Jezeri, Bohemia

A room is safe harbor. No treachery creaks the stair.
I've locked the door; I will not hear them knocking.
Anyone come calling can call themselves blue.

There was a time I liked nothing more than walking
the woods above Vienna, tramping forest paths
to find a patch of green laid square and plush.

I'd sit, tucked in a tapestry of birdsong, and wait
for my breath to settle; let the sun burnish my skin until
the winged horn of the postcoach summoned me home.

And then everything began to sound like
the distant post horn's gleaming trail. . . .

I was careless then, I squandered the world's utterance.
And when my muddy conspirator swayed and quaked
like the tallest poplar tossed by the lightest wind

so that I could *read* his playing, see my score
transcribed on the air, on the breeze—I breathed
his soul through my own fingers and gave up

trying to listen; I watched him and felt
the music—it was better than listening,
it was the last pure sound . . .

(My emperor, emptied of honor,
has crowned himself with gold.)

Why did that savage say it? Why did I hear
what he said, why did I mind what I heard?
Good days, bad days, screech and whistle:

Sometimes I lay my head on the piano
to feel the wood breathing, the ivory sigh.
I know Lichnowski listens some evenings;

he climbs the four flights and hunkers on
the stoop. Odd: I can hear his wheezing
and not this page as it rips—the splitting

so faint a crackle, it could be the last
embers shifting in the grate. . . .

Half-Life

Dull
the days before me,
slack the reins, my horse run off.
What a fable—
to be dunked in kisses,
sprinkled with doubts,
then slathered with high-holy
redundance.

I'm a shadow in sunlight,
unable to blush
or whiten in winter.
Beautiful monster,
where to next—
when you can hear
the wind howl
behind you, the gate

creaking shut?

The foregoing poems, excerpted from *Sonata Mulattica*, published in 2009 by W. W. Norton & Co., form part of a lyric-narrative inspired by a footnote to musical history: In 1803, violinist George Polgreen Bridgetower (1780–1860), wunderkind progeny of a white European woman and a black "African Prince," travels from London to Vienna to meet the continent's "bad boy" musical genius, Ludwig van Beethoven. By all rights, the sonata subsequently inspired by and composed in honor of the mulatto's talents should have borne his name—had not young George, still exuberant from having premiered the difficult piece to great acclaim, become fresh with a girl Ludwig also fancied. Around this crucial moment, Dove builds a passionate, eccentric pageant of eighteenth- and nineteenth-century life— from Haydn's discovery of the dark-skinned child genius in the servants' quarters of a Hungarian castle to Paris right before the French Revolution; from the Prince of Wales' doomed pleasure palace in Brighton to the raucous open air entertainments offered by Vienna's Prater; from Napoleon's ravaged battlegrounds to the self-satisfied refinements of Cambridge. A panoply of luminaries and extras—grave robbers and courtiers, street musicians and aristocrats—populate this grandiose yet melancholy tale.

Our Man in Geneva Wins a Million Euros

Petina Gappah

OUR MAN IN Geneva sits before his computer and blinks at the messages in his in-box.

> *Brother, size matters,* says a message from K. P. Rimmer. *Give her an opportunity to spread rumors about your enormous size. Make her happy by delaying your explosions tonight.*

> *Don't be a two-pump chump,* says Karl Lumsky. *Millions of men are facing this issue, and the smartest ones already got an answer. Safe, efficient, and covering all aspects, Extra-Time will help you forget the premature nightmare.*

> *Do you realize superfluous body kilos kill more and more people around the world?* asks Joni Corona. *We believe that you hate the unattractive look of those people and the social bias against them. Moreover, you've not the will to resist an assault of ruinous eating habits of yours. If it sounds familiar, then we have something for you!*

Our man is the consular officer at the Permanent Mission of the Republic of Zimbabwe to the United Nations office in Geneva, which also serves as the country's embassy to Switzerland. At fifty-five and in his first foreign posting, he is a latecomer to the Internet and all its glories.

"Baba, get e-mail," his children said back in Harare. There was no need, he always said. Too expensive, too set in his ways.

In Geneva, the connection comes with his telephone line. Night after night finds him enmeshed in the World Wide Web, scrolling through e-mails spun in places he has never been, e-mails that are woven into his life and leave him blinking before his computer screen. He types slowly, with two fingers, his tongue between his teeth. "Like a policeman typing a report on a burglary," his wife teases him, "at the Charge Office in Harare."

See how easy communicating becomes, says his daughter, Susan, in England. *Don't forget to send the installment for the next semester.* She follows the sentence with several bouncing bald, yellow, bodiless cartoon heads that open their mouths in toothless smiles as they wink at him.

Baba, I need money, is the echo from his son, Robert, in Canada.

Improve your credit rating, says Frederick Turk.

He is about to click on this message when he sees the next one.

Important communication, this message says, *you are a winner!!* The message is from the European Bank of Luxembourg (EBL) headquarters—Brussels, Belgium. There is an attached letter on the bank's letterhead, signed by Dr. E. S. Rose, Department Head (Corporate Affairs). In a circle around the name are twelve gold stars, just like the stars on the flag of the European Union.

> *Greetings,* Dr. Rose says, *and congratulations. Your e-mail has been entered into the EBL's annual lottery. You have been selected as one of ten winners to win €1,000,000 each. Write back quickly or lose this chance.*

Blood sings from his thumping heart to the rest of his body.

Are you sure that it is me? he types. *I did not enter any lottery. Have I really won a million euros?*

Your e-mail was automatically entered by your Internet service provider, says Dr. Rose. *You really have won a million euros.*

That is the explanation, he thinks, for Rimmer, Lumsky, Corona. And Turk, and Morgan, Shelby, Gordon. They got his e-mail from his Internet service provider.

How do I get the money? he asks.

You will hear from Mr. George, our Chief of Client Accounts.

Within an hour, Mr. George writes and says,

> *Greetings and congratulations. The million is yours to pick up at our offices in Amsterdam. We will charge you an administration fee of €5,000.*

Five thousand euros is a lot of money to pay in admin fees, he thinks, but it is a piffle compared to a million. In his head he does his sums: one euro is roughly two Swiss francs. He has 6,000 francs just sitting in his bank account. It is for Susan's second semester, but it is not due for another month. He can get 4,000 on his credit card to make 10,000. Almost exactly €5,000. This he sees as a sign of a larger truth: God's hand is in this matter, at the very heart of this good fortune.

For the first time in his life, he uses the Internet to book a flight. The secretary at the embassy recommends easyJet. He does not tell her about his bounty; he has not even told his wife. He wants to surprise her and the children with cold-cash evidence of the magnificence of the Lord. His nightly prayers are more fervent than usual. For the Lord has looked upon His servant and found him worthy.

．．．

THE TRIP TO Amsterdam is his first-ever trip out of Geneva. His only travels are when he goes from home in Petit-Saconnex to the embassy in Chambésy, or drives up the gentle incline of the United Nations complex to attend meetings. On Saturdays, he drives his wife across the French border to shop at the Champion hypermarket. On Sundays, they drive to church. Thus he is not so well-flown that he is entirely immune to the thrill of taking off from the ground to be enveloped in the clouds.

The last time that he was on an airplane was on his way to Geneva from Harare where his brothers saw him off at the airport. He has three brothers, one of whom lives in his old house in Waterfalls in Harare. When he calls his brother to check up on him, his family, and the house, his sister-in-law hijacks the conversation with a repetitive litany of woe. Her talk is of power cuts, water cuts, and rising bread prices. "Not like you in Geneva," she says. "*Vagoni muri ku*Switzer."

He tries to inject his own miseries into the conversation. "Can you believe we live in a flat, an apartment, they call it here," he says, too loudly, too vehemently. "Just a flat, heh? A flat, just like single people." Feeling guilty for such a petty complaint. Knowing that at least he has three square meals a day. And electricity that allows him access to the Internet.

It is the grace of God that allowed him to escape the power cuts, the water cuts, the rising bread prices. He is not a career diplomat. God picked him out of the passport office at Makombe Building in Harare, thrusting him out of the way of approaching penury, just in time to enable his children to go to universities in Canada and England. He reads the newspapers that are flown in every month from Harare. He is the least-important member of staff at the embassy, after the secretaries and driver, so he gets them last. The secretaries and driver are local recruits; they do not care about the news from a place they will never call home. The fall in the Zim Dollar does not see a corresponding rise in their blood pressure. So the newspapers end up piled up in his office.

Every editorial wages war against inflation. Government ministers treat it like it is something outside of themselves and their policies; they wage war on it, they proclaim it the public enemy number one, they launch offensives on different fronts. Every week unnamed economists issue sunny predictions on the turnaround of the economy.

Inflation will go down.

From 25,500,000 percent.

Anytime now.

Anytime soon.

The president glowers from every front page.

C. K. Wilde,
Quixotic Ambitions.
2006. Currency collage on panel, 22 x 16 inches. Private Collection, image courtesy of the artist and Pavel Zoubok Gallery

• • •

LIKE SEX SHOPS and pregnant women baring their stomachs in public in the summer, the Internet is a Geneva discovery. He knew of it, of course, but it did not feature much among *his* generation of civil servants. At the passport office in Harare where he was head of the department, everything was handwritten. And even here in Geneva, he does not use the computer at work. All typing is done by the secretary. He does not need the Internet for his work.

Then again, there is very little work.

C. K. Wilde,
Surreal Estate.
2004. Currency
collage, 11 × 8.5
inches. Private
Collection, image
courtesy of the
artist and Pavel
Zoubok Gallery

Geneva is not London, or Johannesburg or Gaborone or Dallas, Texas, where there are hordes of Zimbabweans losing themselves or their passports, dying, and getting arrested. There is not enough consular work to do, and even if there were, he is only a mailbox, an intermediary.

"I will send your papers to Harare," he says to a woman who wants a passport for a newly born Zimbabwean. "It will take up to eight months, in fact, it is faster if you go to Harare and apply from there."

"So what are you here for?" she asks.

"It is faster in Harare," he repeats.

She leaves without saying goodbye.

"In Zimbabwe, out of Zimbabwe, civil servants are all the same," she says.

• • •

HE HAS LEARNED the hard way that a First World lifestyle demands a First World salary. His monthly salary of 6,200 francs a month would be adequate if it were only paid on time. After paying the rent, which is exactly a third of his salary, and paying the bills, and sending money back home, and by living on a diet of Champion value food, he and his wife save enough to put the children through university. Robert is finishing the third year, and Susan only just started.

He has recently been promoted from full-time consular officer to part consular officer and delegate. On seeing him wade through the piled-up newspapers, his ambassador said to him, "Attend meetings at WIPO. And take in ITU and OMM if Chinyanga is busy."

He now spends his days at meeting after meeting at which people talk of compulsory licensing and layout designs and topographies of integrated circuits. They talk of possible amendments to Article 6*quinquies* of the Paris Convention. They talk of the Berne Convention and the Lisbon Convention and trade-related aspects of intellectual property rights. They laugh at jokes that he has no hope of ever understanding.

Other African delegates peel away the veneer of diplomacy on learning his nationality. They address him with an affectionate familiarity. "You Zimbabweans," says the Kenyan delegate. "You want to drive out *muzungu*, heh?" The Kenyan delegate laughs, and the Zambian and Tanzanian delegates join in.

"You Zimbabweans," echoes the Ethiopian delegate. "When are you getting rid of your president? And our Mengistu, there in Harare with him?"

He develops a laugh for encounters such as these.

He learns to fall asleep with his eyes open.

• • •

ON THE FLIGHT to Amsterdam, he dreams of a new geyser for their house in Harare. The last time he called home, his brother's wife said the old geyser is giving problems. He must remember to ask his brother to call Tregers for a quotation, he thinks. Then he remembers that with a million euros, they can buy a new house, *houses*, for him and his brothers. And each of their children. And their children's children.

He works out how much a million euros is in Zimbabwe dollars. Each euro is two million dollars, on the parallel market, of course. Two trillion Zimbabwe dollars. His mind cannot expand enough to take this in.

Twelve zeroes make a billion, according to the United Kingdom system of counting. Twelve zeroes make a trillion, going by the United States version. Two billion or two trillion. One-fifth of Zimbabwe's last annual budget. A lot of money, in any country. In a flood of thanksgiving, he plans all the things he will buy for his Lord's representative on earth, their pastor in Harare.

A new cell phone, for sure.

A stove and a fridge.

A suit for the pastor.

An outfit (with a hat) for the pastor's wife.

Toys and clothes for their children.

In his mind he sees the pastor's children on his farewell visit, peering at the black-and-white cartoon images hissing from their fourth-hand television.

"I will buy them a new television," he vows. "One with a flat screen."

•   •   •

THE GRIMY FAÇADE of the building that houses the European Bank of Luxembourg gives him pause. When he sees the broken elevator, the ten-franc ham sandwich that he ate on the flight moves uneasily in his stomach. He walks up the stairs to the second floor. A door with the letters *EBL* in black flourishes on a gold plaque gives him some reassurance. The door looks serious, solid. Inside, he finds that the offices are not as grimy as the outside indicated. The ham sandwich settles in his innards.

The biggest surprise is Mr. George. He is not the white gentleman of our man's imagination, smiling with largess in a bustling office. Instead, he is a lone young man with a West African accent. He has several gold chains around his neck. He wears black denim jeans with giant pockets at the knees, patent leather shoes, and has two cell phones on his belt. He interrupts their conversation to talk in low tones on his phones. To our man who does not understand the language, the one-sided conversations sound vaguely sinister.

"The money you have won needs to be cleaned," Mr. George explains to him. "And you need to give us 25,000 euros for that purpose." The word sounds like *papas*. "We cannot give it to you in this state." *In dis stet.* "There is an expensive chemical that we must buy." *Iks-pansive kamikal.*

Mr. George takes a fifty-euro note. It has some markings on it, reddish brown, above the stars of Europe. He wipes it down with a cloth on which he has sprinkled a transparent fluid. The note emerges pristine. The term "money laundering" comes from that part of our man's mind that absorbs the news and documentaries that he watches every night on BBC World. He asks the question.

"No, no, no." Mr. George laughs a full-bodied laugh that sees him click-clicking his fingers and clink-clinking his gold chains. "Money laundering. No, no, no. That is for dirty money, money from prostitutes and drugs, money that is sent to accounts in Cayman Islands, you understand me?

This is a lottery, you understand me? This no dirty money. God has chosen us to find people like you, to help you."

Mr. George pauses to answer the phone ringing on his right.

"Dr. Rose, he wants to help you," Mr. George continues. "He even mention your name especially, you understand me?"

Our man understands nothing, but the earlier reference to God settles in his mind. "I am a civil servant," he explains. "I do not have 25,000 euros. Can't you just deduct your money from my million euros before you give it to me?"

Mr. George laughs.

Click-clickety, clink-clinkety.

"No, no, no. That is not how we do it, you understand me? But it's okay. If you don't trust me, we can't do business. You can take your five thousand, and lose your million euros." Our man has already handed over the five thousand euros; it rests snugly in the back pocket of Mr. George's jeans.

He can see its outline when Mr. George turns.

"Here is what I propose. You are a nice guy, flown all this way. You can't leave empty-handed. We can lend it to you. Or rather, we have a partner who can lend it to you." And he mentions a Miss Manning from Equity, Loan, and Finance Company of London. *Lorn-dorn.*

Our man is dismayed to learn that he has to deal with yet another person in yet another city. "You do not have to go to London," Mr. George says. "Miss Manning will contact you to arrange the loan."

Our man is bewildered by all of this. "Why can't the bank just get the money directly from this lender? Why does the money need to be washed?" To all the whys, asked and unasked, Mr. George has one response. "Go back to Geneva, and await Miss Manning's e-mail."

C. K. Wilde,
Alternating
Currency.
1998. Currency collage on paper, 3.75 x 8.25 inches. Private Collection, image courtesy of the artist and Pavel Zoubok Gallery

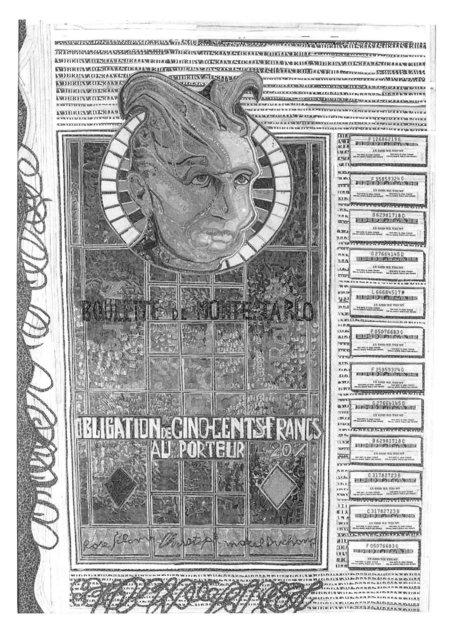

• • •

In Geneva, our man is anxious but not afraid. A week passes, and nothing happens. He e-mails Dr. Rose who tells him to contact Mr. George who tells him to await Miss Manning. Miss Manning finally contacts him, by e-mail and then by post. The letter that comes by post says,

> *Greetings. May our Lord Jesus Christ shower his Blessings upon you and all your Beloved. I looked into my heart and found a Blessed Peace. I pass this Peace on to you today. Herein please find a check for 25,000 euros, to be repaid on receiving your winnings.*

Our man is tempted to kiss the check, but restrains himself. *Worship God, not Mammon.*

Within an hour, Mr. George writes to him.

Greetings, he says. *Please send us the money, as soon as the check clears. Your million will soon be in your account. Trust God.*

In two days, the check clears.

Learn humility, our man chides himself. He promises the Lord not to doubt His wisdom again. He sends the money to Mr. George. He waits a day, two days, a week, two weeks. There is no news from Amsterdam, or Brussels. There is no news from London. *Lorn-dorn.*

He e-mails Dr. Rose, Mr. George, Miss Manning, in that order, every day, twice a day, for one week. Dr. Rose finally responds in a letter of fluid persuasion. *We would not cheat you, my friend*, the e-mail says. *As for me, I am a woman fearful of God. My promise is my credit.*

The reference to the possibility of cheating him does not alarm our man so much as Dr. Rose's revelation that she is a woman. He finds himself back in Amsterdam, Mr. George's voice in his ear. *Dr. Rose, he wants to help you. He even mention your name especially, you understand me?*

You say you are a woman, our man writes. *I thought you were a man. Mr. George distinctly told me that you were a man. In Amsterdam, he said you were a man.*

Make no assumptions my friend, Dr. Rose responds. *Only have faith and all will be well. You will hear from Mr. George.*

Mr. George is brief, to the point.

We need more money for chemicals, he writes. *Miss Manning is sending you another check.*

Our man in Geneva protests, but his e-mails bounce into empty space.

· · ·

EVERY NIGHT, AND first thing in the morning, he sits before the computer. He jumps at the pinging sound that announces new e-mail. He is bothered by a permanent dryness in his throat. Susan calls to remind his wife about her second-semester fees.

"*Wototaura nababa vako*," his wife says. "He will send the money next week, that is, unless he has spent it all." Our man joins in her laughter, his own laugh sounding to his ears like Mr. George's.

"Spent the money? No, no, no."

Click-clickety, clink-clinkety.

He opens his bible to a random page. Like an answer to a prayer, his eyes fall on Jeremiah 33:3. *Call unto me, and I will answer thee, and show thee great and mighty things, which thou knowest not.*

He asks God to show him the way. The Lord speaks to him with all the clarity of common sense. *Forget about the million euros. Come clean to your wife.*

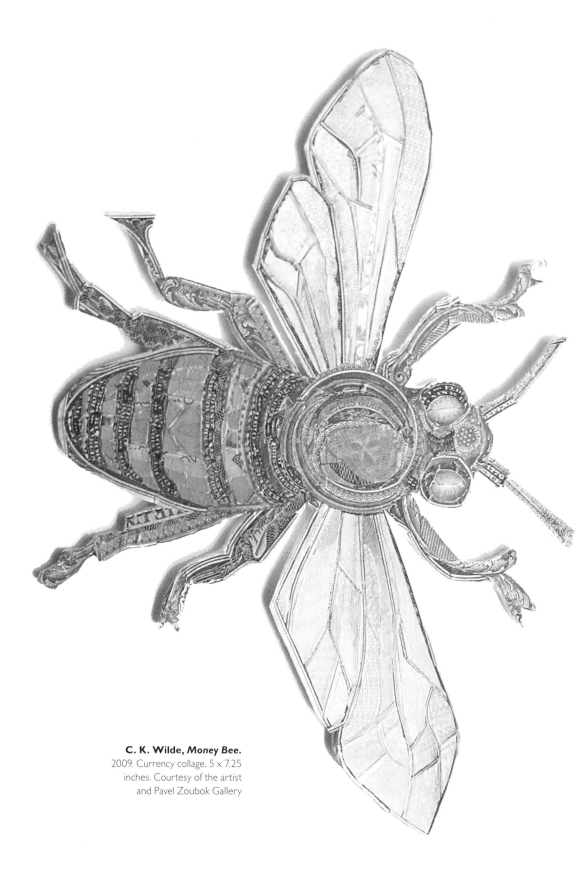

C. K. Wilde, *Money Bee.*
2009. Currency collage, 5 x 7.25
inches. Courtesy of the artist
and Pavel Zoubok Gallery

Pray together and work together. Write a letter to your daughter's university. Ask for a grace period. If necessary, take a loan from those credit people who send e-mails. For the first time in weeks, our man sleeps the sleep of dreamless ease.

He wakes the next day with a sense of purpose. The morning is bright with hope. The clocks have moved up an hour, and the year is approaching spring. As he drives up the hill toward the United Nations, the sun casts its rays through the slits in the giant sculpture of the *Broken Chair* and into the windows of his car. The snow drips from the trees. The birds sing from the melting boughs. At the yellow-and-black zebra crossing just after the *Broken Chair*, he stops to allow a woman and her toddler to cross the street. The child drops its teddy bear, breaks free of its mother, runs back to pick it up, and meets the eyes of our man through the windscreen. The child breaks into a toothless grin and waves. Our man waves back. He is seized by a burst of joy so intense that he almost gasps. As he drives on to Chambésy, he whistles his wife's favorite hymn of thanksgiving. *"Simudza maoko ako, urumbidze Mwari, nekuti Ndiye ega akarurama."*

His heart is filled with grace and gratitude.

In the afternoon, his bank manager asks to see him.

•   •   •

"WE NEED TO discuss an irregular transaction from your account," the bank manager says. "You deposited a fraudulent instrument into your account. We cleared it, but the American bank on which the check was drawn has now refused to honor it.

"We would normally take the blame," the bank manager says, "but this does not apply to checks drawn on American banks."

Our man's stomach turns to water. "Dr. Rose and Mr. George and Miss Manning," he says. "Dr. Rose."

The bank manager offers him a drink. He empties the glass in three swallows. Water dribbles from the glass onto his tie. He explains about the e-mail that started it all, the trip to Amsterdam, the dirty money, the loan, the check. It takes eleven minutes. He contradicts himself three times.

He drinks a liter of water.

"This is clearly a matter for the police," the manager says. "It is difficult to establish identity in such cases. For all we know, this could be the work of just one person. It often is."

The full meaning of the manager's words hits our man. "I can take you to Amsterdam," he says. "We can go there together. I'll pay for our tickets. We can catch Mr. George. Write to Dr. Rose. I have their e-mails. Write to Dr. Rose."

"That is not the bank's immediate concern," the bank manager says. "I called you to give you this." Our man takes the proffered paper. It is a letter of demand. The amount of 51,234 Swiss francs, equivalent to 25,000 euros, is to be repaid within thirty days. He looks at the bank manager's face, looking to find something that says the letter is not real. He does not find what he seeks. He swallows.

From a very far-off place comes a voice that sounds like the bank manager's. The voice sounds like it has traveled a long way and echoes around the room. "I will call the police for you," the voice says.

Police, police, the word is loud in our man's head. His mother's voice speaks across time and space: *You take any more of that sugar, and I will call the police.* That memory sparks another, and suddenly, there they all are; his mother and his uncle Benkias, his sister Shupikai holding his son at age two, all of them crowding his head. "I will call them now," the bank manager says. As the bank manager reaches for the telephone, our man reaches for water, but the glass is empty, the bottle too.⊛

C. K. Wilde

Why cut up money? C. K. Wilde's original idea of currency collage came from Marshall Weber's seminal 1990 show in San Francisco, "The United States of Americana." Weber's collages used real paper currency as manifest socioeconomic semiotic critique. The elegant collages of another American artist, Walter Hamady, further inspired Wilde to engage in collage as a serious artistic practice.

In Wilde's money collages, banknotes are encoded into self-reflexive, critical, multivalent images. The *détournement* or "hijacking" of these symbols allows for the revelation of hidden narratives through a reconfiguration of the symbolic tool of oppression. Within Wilde's currency collages lies a transcript of the powerless, the poor—the victims of the system of global capitalism. Thus, cutting up money represents a disruption of the narrative of economic power. Collage is a way to take an iconic critical stance, through reconfiguring currency and its associated symbols of power.

In 1997, the *Progressive* commissioned Wilde to make several money collages for the magazine, including *Alternating Currency*, which was the first currency collage that he made using bills from all over the world. The piece is a critical reconfiguration of not only the system of capitalism but also the cult of personality propaganda that banknotes represent. Through creating this work, Wilde aimed to provoke deep reflection on the use of symbolic capital as a system of interhuman relations.

Wilde uses banknotes from all eras and nationalities—from failed states and occupying army currencies to the ubiquitous and quotidian U.S. dollar bill. Currency collage can be seen as nostalgia for a time when the symbol of power—money—was still manifest in the physical world. The artist's collages have referenced subjects ranging from space exploration to mythology, religion, slavery, ecology, warfare, the history of money, and art history.

Quixotic Ambitions references Picasso's Don Quixote and Sancho Panza (1955), petroleum production, and warfare. Picasso's windmills are replaced with oil derricks; Don Quixote becomes a mounted World War I–era German soldier occupying Holland. A visual rebus of meanings, redolent with possible symbolic readings, this piece is about art history, nationalism, and the untenable nature of our human desire for control. A compression of historical references into the flat plane of collaged banknote images telescopes the manifold associations found by viewers in this work.

Wilde acknowledges that the ironies of commodifying his dissent through collaged currency are legion: in order to live to make more of these collages, he needs money, so he sells the collages. That the very symbolic manifestation of power has been rendered "useless" as currency in order to create another form of currency is an alchemy of sorts.

The wealthy use my visual critiques of the very system of power that supports our lives as decoration for their homes; art as a cultural icon or a talisman of their political awareness is a wild thicket of ironies. I must confront my own willingness to forget my complicity in the suffering in the world in order to maintain this esoteric practice of making art. Is it ultimately philosophically untenable to justify the production of art objects in a world so troubled? I convince myself that the world needs my work as much as I need it, that by making this work I am participating in the global dialectic of humanity.

—C. K. Wilde

UNIVERSITY OF **PENN**SYLVANIA
PRESS

JOURNAL OF THE HISTORY OF IDEAS

EXECUTIVE EDITORS

Warren Breckman   Martin J. Burke
Anthony Grafton   Ann E. Moyer

Since its inception in 1940, the *Journal of the History of Ideas* has served as a medium for the publication of research in intellectual history that is of common interest to scholars and students in a wide range of fields. It is committed to encouraging diversity in regional coverage, chronological range, and methodological approaches. *JHI* defines intellectual history expansively and ecumenically, including the histories of philosophy, of literature and the arts, of the natural and social sciences, of religion, and of political thought. It also encourages scholarship at the intersections of cultural and intellectual history—for example, the history of the book and of visual culture.

From the October 2008 issue:
Protestant Theology and Apocalyptic Rhetoric in Roger Ascham's *The School Master*,
Ryan J. Stark

The Place of the Sacred in the Absence of God:
Charles Taylor's *A Secular Age*,
Peter E. Gordon

The Idea of Police in Eighteenth-Century England:
Discipline, Reformation, Superintendence,
c. 1780–1800,
F. M. Dodsworth

2009 Subscription Rates
Quarterly
ISSN: 0022-5037
Students: $32
Individuals: $42
Institutions: $115
(International orders,
please add $17 for shipping)

To place a new **subscription** order or renew an existing subscription:

TELEPHONE 717-632-3535, ask for subscriber services

Visit our secure **ONLINE** interface at
http://jhi.pennpress.org

EMAIL requests to
pubsvc@tsp.sheridan.com

Send a **CHECK**, made payable to the "University of Pennsylvania Press" with "JHI70" in the memo line, to
The Sheridan Press
Attn: Penn Press Journals
P. O. Box 465
Hanover, PA 17331

Making Peace with the Sea

one man's life after gun violence in the new South Africa

Rebecca Rosenberg

EARLY SUNDAY MORNING on December 18, 2006, an ambulance carried Luxolo Shihamba to Groote Schuur Hospital in Cape Town, South Africa. The African sun was already hot and bright—in early summer—lighting up Table Mountain and the five-story hospital built into the slope of Devil's Peak. But the ambulance did not continue up the hill along the palm tree–lined road toward the private entrance of the towering neoclassical building. Instead, it made an abrupt left turn and drove up a concrete ramp to the hospital's public entrance.

The paramedics placed Luxolo, twenty-three years of age, on a stretcher and wheeled him past the drab beige walls of the hallway into the resuscitation unit. One paramedic told Dr. Clair Neser, a second-year resident, that Luxolo had been shot in the neck with a .22 caliber gun. "He appears stable," reported the paramedic. "He was conscious and alert the whole way."

Luxolo, whose name means *peace* in Xhosa, had been transferred from Mitchell's Plain Day Hospital, which has about 200 beds, serves a population of 1.2 million, and doesn't have an x-ray machine. Anyone in Cape Town who needs an x-ray, an MRI, or a serious operation, as did Luxolo, is referred to Groote Schuur, one of the country's top three teaching hospitals. It was here where Chris Barnard performed the first heart transplant in the world.

Neser helped log roll six-foot-tall Luxolo onto a hospital bed. The paramedics and two nurses held Luxolo on his side while the resident snapped on a surgical glove, smeared her index finger with KY Jelly, and inserted it into his rectum. "Poor rectal tone," she noted. Though his blood pressure was a little low, his vitals were stable.

She asked the patient, "Are you in pain?"

"Man, my neck is sore," Luxolo replied. The darkness of his bald head and face contrasted with the whites of his eyes, which were surprisingly alert.

"What happened?" she asked, as she looked at the paramedic's notes.

"I was shot in the neck," he explained. "This guy thought I stole his mobile phone."

The supervising doctor, Christian Bremm, entered the room, and Neser pointed to Luxolo's erection.

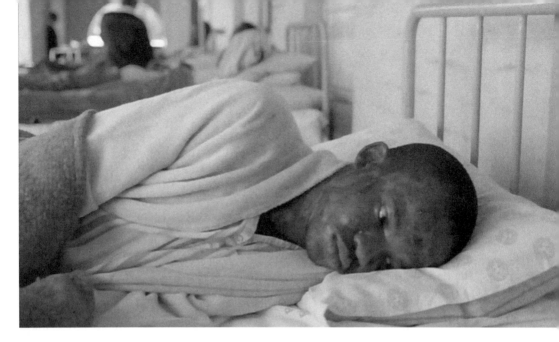

"Not good: priapism, no rectal tone, he's not moving his legs—he looks paralyzed," she said.

Yesterday (2004), directed by Darrell James Roodt

Bremm nodded. (A priapism is a nonsexual and—for people with sensation—painful erection that often appears after a spinal cord injury.)

Neser took a pin and poked Luxolo's left foot, then asked, "Does this feel sharp or blunt?"

"I don't feel it," Luxolo answered.

The resident then struck his left and right ankles, calves, shins, knees, thighs, and lower abdomen. Each time the answer was the same: "I don't feel it."

She asked him to squeeze her hand; his grip was weak. Neser ordered an MRI, which later revealed swelling and compression of the spine. Three hours after Luxolo was admitted, the neurosurgeon examined him, recording in his chart: "complete spinal cord injury: prognosis poor."

The resuscitation room was empty except for a nurse who was filling out paper work, and a visiting German medical student at Luxolo's side. The student cleaned the blood and dirt from the entry wound and, with a strange mixture of eagerness and trepidation, used a curved needle to puncture the skin; then, hesitating a moment, he pulled the thread through. Luxolo looked the other way—he didn't like the sight of blood. It was the student's first time suturing a live person.

Meanwhile, Luxolo's mother, Nomsa Shihamba, and his fiancée (whom he refers to as his wife), Mandisa Ompopo, sat in the waiting room. They had followed the ambulance from Mitchell's Plain Day Hospital. A doctor there told them that Luxolo might be paralyzed. In the waiting room, time was lost and everything seemed to stop for Nomsa. For Mandisa, the situation was still too fresh and dreamlike for her to be able to acknowledge its gravity. But they both hoped, albeit for different reasons, that the doctor was wrong and that Luxolo would walk again.

Later that day, Luxolo was transferred to trauma ward C12. His situation was by no means rare. A lot of patients, Neser indicated, came in with serious gunshot wounds inflicted during arguments over something as trivial as a cell phone. "A kid came in just the other night," she said. "He was stabbed over a Savannah [alcoholic cider]."

• • •

I MET LUXOLO the day he was admitted. I had come to the hospital to try to understand violence in the country. South Africa has the second-highest homicide rate and the highest number of reported rapes in the world, according to the United Nations and Statistics South Africa. The resuscitation unit, a section of the surgical emergency room equipped to handle severe traumas, treated 1,500 gunshot patients and 5,000 assault patients in 2006. Most minor gunshot wounds are treated at the local day hospital. The life-threatening and complex cases are transferred to the resuscitation unit. In the same week that Luxolo came in, a teenager was stabbed in the heart with a screwdriver; a mother of three children was shot in the head by her boyfriend; a middle-aged man was attacked with an ax; and a teenager was beaten to death by his neighbors after having stolen a CD. Three of these cases had something in common: the victims were high on crystal meth, known as *tik* in South Africa. While overall crime has decreased slightly over the last decade, tik-related violent crime has doubled. Although Luxolo wasn't high on tik, his shooting was connected to the drug.

South Africa has the second-highest homicide rate and the highest number of reported rapes in the world.

• • •

TWO DAYS AFTER his admission, Luxolo sat in a hospital bed in the general trauma ward. It was late, about 9:00 PM, and the lights were dimmed. One of the nurses was playing solitaire on the hospital computer; another eyed me suspiciously from across the room. After a few minutes, she pulled me aside and told me that I should call Luxolo by his alias, *Elton*. When Nomsa came in the day before, she said she didn't want anyone to find out where her son was. She worried that the shooter would hear that he was still alive and try to kill him.

"I like him," the nurse said. "The doctors said his prognosis is poor, but don't tell him. It's important for him to have hope."

Luxolo was reading (in Xhosa) Psalm 100 from the Book of Psalms. He said it was his favorite. He translated the passage, as he understood it, into English:

Praise the Lord,
and the whole world should praise the Lord,
and you should be happy when you do it.
Come before him humble, because he is the Lord,
who is good and kind.

The next day, Luxolo's bed was moved to the other side of the ward. Only three of the ward's twelve beds were occupied. Situated diagonally from Luxolo was a middle-aged man with a head injury. His eyes had a wild look, and he kept jerking his body erratically. The nurses had tied his right hand to the bed's metal railing with a diaper pad to stop him from pulling out his IV. The man was shredding the pieces of the diaper's white fluff with his other hand and dropping them onto the floor.

"He's crazy," Luxolo explained.

Luxolo made friends with another patient, Lusanda Jakuja, a thin nineteen-year-old with a small gold hoop in his right ear. He was missing most of the teeth on the sides of his jaw, and the front two had black cavities. He said that he had eaten too much *snoek* [smoked white fish], and smiled to show me the damage. "See," he said pointing to his teeth. When he smiled, his thick lips curled up more on the left side than on the right, creating a mischievous, playful expression. Admitted the day after Luxolo, Lusanda had also suffered a spinal cord injury, having been stabbed in the neck when he tried to mediate an argument between two friends.

Luxolo appreciated Lusanda's company and was in reasonable spirits but had grown weary of sitting in the hospital all day and just wanted his legs to heal so that he could leave. All he had for entertainment was his bible and the hospital's television, with its two fuzzy channels. He wanted to go outside, so I placed his catheter bag, filled with dark yellow urine, on his lap and

Yesterday (2004), directed by Darrell James Roodt

wheeled the heavy bed the half mile to the visitor's entrance. (The hospital is color-coded to orient visitors and staff because it's so large.) From the edge of the concrete parking lot, Luxolo could see the mountains and the rays of the late-afternoon sun hitting the green trees in the courtyard. When I asked him what had happened the night he was shot, he changed the subject. He wanted to know about the United States and asked whether I had ever met the rappers Biggie and Snoop Dogg.

On Christmas Day, Luxolo's mother, fiancée, daughter, and sister arrived. They had visited every day—often twice a day—since he was admitted. His mother, a heavy-set woman, wore a bright green shirt, blue jeans, and black-rimmed glasses. His fiancée, Mandisa, whose name means *pretty*, seemed cool and withdrawn. She wore a long black wig and a short green dress that hugged her narrow waist and the curve of her round hips. She sat in a chair, her face tight and hard, spoon-feeding Luxolo home-cooked chicken and rice without saying more than a few words.

All he had for entertainment was his bible and the hospital's television, with its two fuzzy channels.

Meanwhile, Luxolo joked with Lusanda (his new friend) and played with his two-year-old daughter, Uyathanewa, who was yanking on his catheter and slobbering on the bed's metal railings. The family called her "Sissy," and she had the same dark eyes, thick eyebrows, and stocky build as her father. She looked much older than her two years—perhaps even five. Her white princess dress with a bow at the back, a Christmas gift from that morning, was already soiled. Luxolo's twelve-year-old sister, Senele, stood in the corner quietly practicing her hip-hop dance moves. After Nomsa gave birth to her last child, she said to herself "*Senele* [enough]," and that became her daughter's name.

Standing a few feet away from Luxolo, Nomsa spoke softly, her face strained. "The doctors told me he's paralyzed, but I have hope," she said. "He says he can move his toes and has sensation." A few days earlier, Nomsa had filed a police report on behalf of her son.

In the United States, when a person comes into a hospital with a gunshot wound, the hospital is legally required to notify the police. In South Africa, no one at the hospital calls the police, even if the patient requests it. The victim and his family must do the work. Before Christmas, Nomsa went to the Mitchell's Plain police station. An investigator was assigned to the case, and he asked Nomsa to bring him the names and addresses of her son's attackers. In block letters on a piece of paper, she wrote the name of the alleged shooter, Ntsikelelo Madikane, and his alleged accomplice, Bandile. The men were usually together and lived in a shack in Khayelitsha, a squatter camp of about 1 million people. When Nomsa returned to the police station on December 22 to check on the case, she was told that it was on hold until the investigating officer returned from his two-week holiday.

After Luxolo's family had left, a nurse wheeled him to the other end of the ward. He pulled out a cigarette from under his blanket and asked, "Sister, can

I please have a light?" She shook her head, opened the window and replied in Afrikaans, "*Boetie* [Brother], smoking is bad for you." Then she passed him a plastic cup filled with water and reached over to light his cigarette.

The soft evening light spilled in from the window and cast a shadow on the right side of Luxolo's face. For the next two hours, he spoke freely about his life. He came from an upper-middle-class family and always lived in a proper home with running water and electricity, a luxury for Africans. To Lusanda, who grew up in a shack, Luxolo was a wealthy man. Nomsa was a schoolteacher, working toward a Ph.D. on HIV/AIDS, and his older sister was an accountant. In the new South Africa, Luxolo had every opportunity for success. But, Luxolo said, his mind was too lazy for school.

As a young teenager, Luxolo stole white people's cars with his friends. His mother had to bring him before the juvenile court three times, but each of the cases was dropped: no evidence or witnesses.

"I was always lucky," he admitted.

His mother did not reprimand Luxolo when he got into trouble. In fact, he couldn't remember a single incident in which she punished him after the age of twelve. Nomsa said she had forgotten about the car thefts, and, aside from that, Luxolo had always been a good boy. In African society, mothers are usually not in a position to be able to discipline their sons. In the absence of a father, a young teenage boy often becomes the man of the house, even when he continues to act like a child.

At age sixteen, Luxolo dropped out of school. He had already started dating Mandisa, who tried to persuade him to finish, but he wouldn't listen. His mother expressed disapproval but felt powerless to do much more. For several years, Luxolo smoked and sold Mandrax, an addictive narcotic that was once widely used in Africa as a painkiller. He quit dealing by the age of eighteen, but continued to steal VW Golfs. He would take the stolen cars to his childhood friend, Lerato Skefile, who lived in his grandmother's large two-garage house down the street, and together they'd break them apart. When Lerato's grandmother died and left him the house, it became a hangout for the neighborhood teenagers. The year before he was shot, Luxolo spent almost every weekend and many weekdays at Lerato's house.

Her white princess dress with a bow at the back, a Christmas gift from that morning, was already soiled.

The street leading into Mandalay splits to the left and the right in front of the house, eventually rejoining to form a circle. Lerato's house is one of the largest and most visible in Mandalay, and Nomsa must pass whenever she leaves or returns home. Most of the neighborhood homes are well maintained, but not Lerato's, which has empty Coca-Cola cans, beer bottles, and candy wrappers strewn across the yard. Painted a light pink shade, the house is surrounded by a low brick wall, and has a metal gate that opens onto a paved driveway.

About a year before his injury, Luxolo had started a tik-selling business with Lerato. Luxolo had an in. His Afrikaans being particularly good, he was able to negotiate deals with the colored gangs in control of trade. (*Colored* is the official term for mixed-race South Africans.) Luxolo and Lerato gave the gangs cars in exchange for tik and marijuana, which they then sold.

The first week in the hospital had given Luxolo time to think about his relationship with Lerato and the sequence of events that led to the shooting. He realized that there was much more to the incident than a cell phone.

• • •

ON DECEMBER 14, Luxolo was at Lerato's house with about fifteen other people drinking, listening to music, and smoking weed. Ntsikelelo and Bandile, whom Luxolo knew from grade school, were visiting the house for the first time. That night, Ntsikelelo said that his cell phone had been stolen from his car. He was visibly angry, but Luxolo didn't think much of it at the time and went home.

The next evening, just before midnight, Luxolo returned to the house and chatted with an acquaintance who was sitting outside. The acquaintance said that Ntsikelelo and Bandile had come to the house earlier that day with guns and were speaking to Lerato about Luxolo, who they thought had stolen the cell phone. After the chat, Luxolo went inside and saw Lerato. Hours passed, but Lerato didn't mention the angry visitors.

In the absence of a father, a young teenage boy often becomes the man of the house, even when he continues to act like a child.

"This is my friend, and he doesn't tell me people with guns are looking for me?" Luxolo asked.

On the afternoon of December 16, Luxolo took his daughter to the house to play with Lerato's son. It was a hot afternoon, and Luxolo was throwing Sissy in the air and catching her. Meanwhile, someone inside the house heard Lerato answer the phone and say, "Not now. He's with his baby girl."

Though Luxolo felt something wasn't right, he couldn't pin it down. He left and returned alone on the evening of December 17, at about 11:00 PM. On the way, he remembered thinking to himself, "I shouldn't go here anymore—this house is a dirty place." He parked his white VW Golf next to the lawn just inside the metal gate. About ten people were sitting in the living room. Not fifteen minutes after Luxolo had arrived, Ntsikelelo pulled up with Bandile. In retrospect, Luxolo suspected that someone at the house called to tell them that he had arrived. He wondered whether it was Lerato.

When Ntsikelelo walked in, Luxolo turned to him and said in Xhosa, "My brother, my friend, I hear I stole your cell phone?"

Yesterday (2004), directed by Darrell James Roodt

"Let's talk outside," Ntsikelelo responded.

Standing on the lawn, Ntsikelelo demanded his cell phone as he thrust the palms of his hands against Luxolo, who stumbled backward.

Luxolo remembered saying, "No, man, I didn't steal it." This made Ntsikelelo even angrier, and he threatened to take the stereo from his car. "Fuck you, man, take my music. I didn't steal your cell phone," Luxolo shouted.

They screamed and swore at each other, the pitch of their voices rising. "Come on, you guys grew up together, don't be boys, you can work this out," Bandile said, trying to mediate.

As Luxolo walked back toward the house, toward the thumping bass of the music playing in the living room, Ntsikelelo yelled, "Hey Biggie!"

Luxolo turned as he heard a gun cocking, then saw the barrel of a .22 caliber gun three feet from his face. Ntsikelelo fired four times. A bullet burrowed down the right side of Luxolo's neck, exiting near his left shoulder blade. It was the only shot to hit him. His body softened like putty and collapsed onto the dirt ground, blood seeping into the hard earth. People in the house dashed out the front door to see what had happened, while Ntsikelelo and Bandile rushed to their car and drove off. Lerato and two other men picked up Luxolo and placed him in the backseat of his VW Golf. Blood poured from his neck onto the backseat of the car. Although he felt sore, Luxolo wasn't in much pain and was completely alert. Lerato drove to the Mitchell's Plain Day Hospital and left Luxolo at the front entrance, then drove the car back to the house and parked it on the curb outside the gate. The car's backseat was saturated with wet blood. Lerato didn't call the police, Nomsa, or Mandisa.

"My heart is so pure, I have no hatred," Luxolo said calmly. "I don't hold things against people."

But Luxolo did have a lot of questions and the time to ponder over them. He wanted to know why Ntsikelelo had shot him. Was it really over a cell phone? The more he thought about it, the more he suspected that his childhood friend Lerato had set him up. He later heard from another friend that Lerato had told Ntsikelelo that he saw Luxolo steal the cell phone.

"Do I look like some crook who'd steal a mobile phone?" Luxolo asked.

After a few minutes of reflection, Luxolo became a little less forgiving and said he'd like to put Lerato in the trunk of his car, drive to the highest cliff, and push him off. No guns or knives, though—he doesn't like the sight of blood.

• • •

LUXOLO HAD SURMISED that Lerato wanted him dead—that he became greedy and wanted the tik and car business to himself. There had been signs. Lerato had become cooler lately, and they hadn't been talking much. None of Luxolo's friends visited him in the hospital, but he was okay with it. "Most of them are pretenders," he said. "I was shot in front of them. They obviously knew I was going to get shot."

The sun had set, and the hospital ward was darker. The conversation had exhausted Luxolo, and he was wheeled back to his spot near the TV, across from Lusanda, who was complaining about the soreness in his legs.

Luxolo turned as he heard a gun cocking, then saw the barrel of a .22 caliber gun three feet from his face. Though Lusanda's chart indicated a spinal cord injury, its severity wasn't yet known. When Lusanda talked about the things he'd do as soon as he could walk again, Luxolo laughed, "You're never going to walk; you can't even move your toes." At the time, Luxolo was able to wiggle three toes on his left foot, which Lusanda could not do.

Luxolo and Lusanda were both waiting for spaces to open at the Western Cape Rehabilitation Centre. But Luxolo had a problem. He had developed a severe bedsore from lying in the same spot all day, and the rehab center wouldn't take him until it healed. One of the medical students carved out the tissue around the sore to clean it and accelerate the healing. The nurses needed to turn him every two hours; otherwise, the fist-size wound would grow wider and deeper. But they didn't have the time. The next day, Lusanda was transferred, and Luxolo asked one of the nurses to try to persuade the rehab center to take him, too. She did so by claiming that the sore had healed. Less than twenty-four hours later, Luxolo was also transferred.

The Western Cape Rehabilitation Centre was built in 2004, on the grounds of Lentegeur Psychiatric Hospital. This government rehab facility is the only one in the Western Cape and is probably the best equipped in the country. Once the facility accepts a patient, there is a waiting period of

from two weeks to two months. After passing through the main gate of the *Yesterday* (2004), directed by Darrell James Roodt psychiatric hospital, it's about a mile and a half to the rehab entrance at the northeast corner of the grounds. On a warm day, patients stroll along the road carrying their IVs and chest-tube drains. The center is made up of four beige brick buildings with red-tiled roofs, and its main entrance is flanked by palm trees and surrounded by purple flowers. Visitors would hardly know that beyond the ten-foot walls that enclose the massive grounds lies a vast stretch of dangerous shantytowns.

Luxolo and Lusanda were placed in Ward E, in rooms down the hall from each other. Many of the patients have never lived in a proper building with plumbing, electricity, or even furniture. For many, it's the nicest place they've ever stayed. "Some of the patients don't want to leave," remarked administrator David Roodt. "Many live in shacks without water or electricity. If they're in a wheelchair, they can't navigate the rocks and paths of Khayelitsha." Lusanda is from one of the Khayelitsha shantytowns.

Returning home will probably be easier for Luxolo. Roodt, who has worked at a government rehab facility for more than fifteen years, said that more and more patients are coming in with injuries like Luxolo's: "It used to be stabbings, and now it's guns." Almost half the patients become paralyzed after being shot, stabbed, or assaulted; car accidents, sports and other injuries account for the other half. Government rehabs don't, however, collect more detailed data and so do not know the number of patients who have been shot or stabbed.

• • •

ON JANUARY 3, 2007, Luxolo was lying in bed staring at the wall to his left. He wasn't smiling, he wouldn't say more than a few words, and he was in a lot of pain. As swelling in his spine decreased, the nerves all over his body became hypersensitive. "My arms are bloody sore," he said. "The doctor said my nerves are confused."

For almost three weeks, Luxolo had been lying in bed and still could wiggle only three toes. He couldn't sit in a wheelchair or start physical therapy because of his bedsore, and the administrators were annoyed that he was taking up space when he couldn't yet participate in the program. Lusanda, on the other hand, was progressing well. He spent his days in a wheelchair zooming along the concrete pathways that connected the four wards. His legs were getting stronger, and he could lift them a few inches. He even befriended a young woman—she had become paraplegic after a jealous boyfriend shot her in the back.

Almost half the patients become paralyzed after being shot, stabbed, or assaulted.

From bed, Luxolo and the two other patients in his room could watch Lusanda wheeling himself down the hallway and back-chatting the nurses. "He's such a child—he needs to go to the bush," Luxolo said. In the Xhosa tribe, teenagers become men when they are sent to the bush and circumcised without painkillers. Mandisa said that when Luxolo went to the bush at the age of twenty-one, he changed. "He was violent before," she said. "He was in a lot of fights"—that was how he got his nickname, *Biggie*, the name Ntsikelelo called out just before he shot him.

Luxolo was a little despondent, and he wanted more than anything to sit outside and stare at the light blue Boland Mountains on the horizon. From the window behind his head, he could feel the warmth of the sun, but he could not see it. The wheels on his bed didn't work properly, so the nurses couldn't easily move him. "I visit him every day," Mandisa said. "I can see he's not as positive and strong, but I think he's trying. I just want him to walk."

Nomsa arrived with chicken stew and fed Luxolo bite by bite. She wore a large green shirt, which covered the zipper of the jeans she could no longer zip up. Her eyes drooped from fatigue. "All of us, we've been traumatized," she said of the family. "It's not been easy. We live in fear in this country." A few days earlier, Nomsa's friend had told her something troubling. Someone who had been at Lerato's house around the time Luxolo was shot said that Ntsikelelo warned everyone that if the police got involved, he'd shoot Luxolo's whole family. Nomsa was concerned, but her safety was less important to her than making sure that the man who shot her son was punished.

After the incident, Nomsa decided that she had to sell her house and move; she no longer felt safe in Mandalay. At night, she even thought that she was being followed. She guessed that it was one of Ntsikelelo's friends trying to intimidate her for going to the police. She called the investigating officer, Michael Nkenke, but he said there was nothing he could do without proof. Mandisa was also worried. She was driving the white VW that she had given Luxolo, and she thought that she was being followed. She worried that the men who shot Luxolo would come after her. She even had the plates changed. "Who knows what he used that car for?" Mandisa explained. Early that afternoon, Mandisa arrived at the rehab center wearing a pink headscarf with a hole in it, and a thin chiffon red dress that clung to her flat tummy and shapely breasts. Luxolo's eyes scanned his fiancée's figure, but he said nothing.

Yesterday (2004), directed by Darrell James Roodt

• • •

NOMSA'S FRIEND CHRIS MANDESA made an appointment for Nomsa and Mandisa at a *sangoma*, a traditional African healer, and they took me along. The sangoma lives and works in Khayelitsha Site B, a neighborhood that has an unemployment rate above 50 percent. As we drove, we passed thousands of densely packed shacks made of corrugated aluminum and painted in bright reds, oranges, blues, and purples. A few stones weighing a roof down was all that held a shack together. Rain often leaked through the roofs, and it looked as though a strong wind could blow them over like dominos.

Khayelitsha, which means *new home*, was created during apartheid for a small number of African migrants from the Eastern Cape who had been granted permission to work in the region. Blacks without permits weren't allowed to live in urban areas such as Cape Town, which had been predominantly white and colored. When apartheid ended, Africans from the Eastern Cape flooded into Khayelitsha in search of work, building shacks out of tin and cardboard. During the first post-apartheid elections, the African National Congress (ANC) pledged to build homes for everyone. But when the party came to power, rampant corruption and the overwhelming number of people in need of adequate shelter and basic services made delivery of this promise difficult. (The white government of the National Party answered to about 4 million people, while the ANC had to answer to 40 million.) Despite a booming economy, there is a severe shortage of low-income homes, while the rapid construction of luxury buildings along the Atlantic seaboard, fueled by foreign investors, has glutted that market.

She worried that the men who shot Luxolo would come after her. She even had the plates changed.

Driving along the paved road that runs through the middle of the squatter camp, we passed dozens of children playing barefoot in the street. A woman walking on the side of the road balanced a ten-pound bag of maize on her head as she passed beneath a tangled mess of telephone wires and laundry lines.

Nomsa parked at the curb, and we walked down a dirt path, past strewn candy wrappers and broken glass from beer and vodka bottles, to the sangoma's shack. The temperature was in the low 100s (Fahrenheit) and the orange powdery dust stuck to the sweat on our bodies. Inside the shack, a jovial fat man in his sixties sat behind a makeshift desk; whenever he laughed, which was often, his stomach jiggled. He had a one-toothed grin like that of an infant, and his uneven bald head made him look like a Buddha. When he saw Sissy, he greeted her, "Hello little *gogga* [an endearing term for a child, which literally means *insect*]," and passed her the purple Fanta he was drinking. Three grandmothers sat on a bench to his left eating Hungry Lion Chicken from a box.

Dozens of flies buzzed around the dirt-floored shack, landing on everyone's feet. They crawled across Sissy's face, but she didn't chase them off. As soon as Sissy saw one of the women pull out a drumstick, she rushed to it, her arm outstretched, and her eyes opened widely—she wasn't asking; she was demanding.

The sangoma identified himself as Dr. D. V. M. Jonga of Emavundleni Herbal Clinic. His pale pink office, cluttered with mayonnaise jars filled with rusting bolts, chili powder, or bundles of twigs and bark, was no more than ten feet wide. On the sangoma's desk was a basketball-sized cabbage head, the leaves wilting in the heat, and a yellow-speckled squash. The sangoma did not speak English and so asked Chris to translate from Xhosa for me. The grandmothers were waiting for their appointment after Nomsa and Mandisa.

After Nomsa explained the situation, Jonga put his hands together as if in prayer and closed his eyes to listen to the ancestors whisper in his ear. According to Xhosa tradition, the ancestors control people's destinies. The

Yesterday (2004), directed by Darrell James Roodt

sangoma leaned back, his mouthslightly agape, revealing the one crooked tooth on his lower jaw as he pointed toward the rusted ceiling. Wrapping his hands around his neck as though another person were choking him, he slid down in his chair, apparently struggling with the spirits. The ancestors explained that Luxolo should be able to walk again. "If you injure your hand, you can't have pains in your ears," Jonga said, repeating the words of the ancestors. "If your injury is on your neck, your bottom body can't just be paralyzed."

After communing more with the spirits, Jonga was told what to prescribe for Luxolo. "We're using this ammonium chloride," he said. "It's a white herb you just put on your tongue. It treats internal bleeding, internal injuries, and stabilizes pains." Nomsa had a knee problem, and the sangoma said that the powder could treat that condition, too. He suggested another potion to improve Nomsa's fortune: "If you mix red and white root and stir it, you get foam. If you drink that water you can vomit—it brings you big luck."

He said that he even had a cure for HIV/AIDS, but it wasn't mixed yet. In Khayelitsha, one in ten people and one in three pregnant women are infected with the virus. Treatment for HIV/AIDS has been controversial in South Africa after the (then) national health minister, Manto Tshabalala-Msimang, said that eating beets and garlic and relying on traditional African medicine, such as the remedies recommended by sangomas, was better than using antiretrovirals. Jonga picked up a bag of the ammonium chloride, which is sold in blocks at hardware stores, and passed it to one of the grandmothers to try. As soon as it hit her tongue, her face grimaced, and her eyes began to tear. Ammonium chloride is a slightly acidic salt used in many products, including cleaning solutions, plywood glue, and shampoo.

Yesterday (2004), directed by Darrell James Roodt

Jonga handed Mandisa a yellow Ziploc bag of the white powder and a piece of bark, which she was instructed to grate. She was to administer one tablespoon of each to Luxolo. There was no charge for the visit. Sangomas ask for payment only when the treated person shows improvement, and it is rare for people to cheat the healers because it is believed that this would cause a curse on them and their families.

Before we left, the sangoma wanted to show me the books he studied. He brought out an English anatomy book and proudly flipped the pages. He couldn't read English, so he had to rely on the color diagrams. Nomsa and Mandisa deferentially thanked Jonga. Xhosas believe that the ancestors must call a person to become a sangoma. Luxolo said that he had been called and would study to become a sangoma when he was healed.

In the car, Chris explained how he had learned of Jonga. Doctors had told a professor friend of his who had been in a car accident that he would be permanently paralyzed from the neck down. Jonga prescribed an ointment for the man, and, according to Chris, "After not even three minutes that guy woke up and got out of bed in the ICU. I don't say that what he gave us will heal the boy, but it will do its measure."

Back at Nomsa's house, Mandisa's head sweated as she grated the hard bark into a plastic bowl. The fine powders drifted into the air, causing her to break into a violent cough. The powder was everywhere: on the dining room table, on the white-tiled floor, even on the window's lace curtains. The house was large, and the living room had a cloth couch set; children's toys were scattered across the floor. The wood entertainment center had dozens of framed pictures of Nomsa's children and grandchildren.

His pale pink office, cluttered with mayonnaise jars filled with rusting bolts, chili powder, or bundles of twigs and bark, was no more than ten feet wide.

Sissy was in the corner playing with her cousin. Though the same age, Sissy was six inches taller, with the physique of a wrestler. Mandisa handed Sissy a bottle. Then Sissy watched as her mother handed her cousin a bottle. When Mandisa turned, Sissy snatched the bottle from her cousin, tucked it under her arm, and quickly waddled away. Her delicate cousin wailed in frustration. Nomsa gave the cousin back her bottle, and laughed, "She's a bully." It was hard to look at Sissy and not see Luxolo in her face, Mandisa said.

While Nomsa was in the kitchen, Luxolo called Mandisa on her cell phone. She ignored it. She said he sometimes called ten times in a row. "He's feeling insecure," she said. "He asks what I'm doing all the time. He told Chris's son to watch me."

Upon arriving at the hospital, Mandisa checked to make sure that none of the nurses were nearby and fed Luxolo a spoon of the ammonium chloride. He scrunched up his face as though he had eaten a lemon, shook his head and exclaimed, "Water! Water!" which he gulped down as soon as it

Yesterday (2004), directed by Darrell James Roodt

arrived. Then Mandisa fed him a tablespoon of the dry, rough bark, which scraped against Luxolo's throat. He immediately began to choke and break into a violent cough. He pounded on his chest and turned red, trying to clear it. It took several minutes for the irritation to subside. "African medicine never tastes good," he said. "But it works."

The staff doesn't like patients to take sangoma medicine, but it's a problem that is difficult to control at many South African hospitals. "We've had witchdoctors who gave patients battery acid and bleach that burned the esophagus," relayed administrator David Roodt. "They get really sick, and we have to go ask the family, *What happened?*" Usually, these medications cause more problems than they cure, he said.

Luxolo said that he already felt better from the medication—he could feel it working. A couple of days later, Luxolo was lying on the trolley that he'd been asking the nurse for every day. It was a long, flat bed, with two bicycle-sized wheels at the front and two smaller wheels at the back. The nurses tied his legs down with a sheet that read: *Property of the Western Cape Province: Removal is Illegal.* About a year ago, the hospitals realized that they were losing millions of rands each year from linen theft, which prompted them to print warnings on all of the sheets.

The trolley was large and difficult to maneuver even with normal strength, but Luxolo had been in bed for weeks, so the muscles in his arms had weakened. He could wheel himself only a few feet before he got tired and needed to rest. He rolled himself to the recreation room about forty feet from his bed and parked in front of an upright wood piano. It was out of tune, and the light brown paneling on the side was peeling. Using his index fingers as though he were typing, Luxolo made up songs for more than two hours. Over the next few weeks, playing the piano became his favorite way to pass the time. "When I get back, I'm going to ask the old man in my neighborhood to teach me," he said. "I often walk past and hear music from his house. He said he'd teach me once, but I never went."

It was afternoon, and Mandisa hadn't visited yet. "I phoned her thirty times, and she didn't answer," he said. Mandisa slept late. At night, she felt nervous and had difficulty falling asleep. Her doctor had prescribed sedatives.

The nurses put Luxolo back in bed by early afternoon. He was tired, and his arms hurt. Next to his bed was a chunk of driftwood, and he was **The powder was** fidgeting with a piece of seaweed, dried in the **everywhere: on the dining** shape of a leafless tree that looked like the wind had blown all its branches east. He had asked **room table, on the white-** Mandisa to bring these things from their home. **tiled floor, even on the** "The first thing I want to do when I leave here is drive to the sea and just chill and talk to my **window's lace curtains.** ancestors," he said. In Xhosa culture, the sea is a holy place, where the ancestors live. He asked if I had ever been to Monwabisi Beach. He said that it was beautiful, that he loved to sit on the sand dunes there and stare at the waves.

Luxolo said that he had dreamt about the ocean the previous night:

> I was there, my mother was there. I was with the police. I was in a car—it drove over and fell. I wasn't hurt. I was trying to get to this place to get *muti* [herbal medicine]. We were standing on top of this cliff, and the sea was below, and the people were scared. The sea was lovely, though it was scary.

Luxolo dreamt a lot about the ocean.

• • •

LATER IN THE afternoon, I told Mandisa that I wanted to meet Luxolo's friend Lerato. She said that it wasn't safe to go alone, but she would take me. We parked on the curb and Lerato let us in through a side gate. Two teenagers were standing near the brick wall chasing after Lerato's one-and-a-half-year-old baby. Lerato was distracted, holding a baby bottle in one hand and a pacifier in the other. He had a four-inch vertical scar to the left of his eye. The two teenagers were eyeing me. Lerato didn't look at me as he spoke.

He recounted his own version of the night that Luxolo was shot. He said that Luxolo had parked outside the gate, and the moment he arrived, even before he came into the yard, the two men came for him and shot him. Luxolo had said that he had parked inside the driveway and was hanging out for at least ten minutes before Ntsikelelo and Bandile arrived.

Lerato pointed just outside the metal gate, indicating, "That's where Luxolo was shot. I looked at them, they were talking. Then I turned around, and the next thing I knew, they shot him." Luxolo didn't realize that Lerato had seen the shooting. As I stood next to Lerato, the metal gate slid open, and a white BMW accelerated and swerved toward me as though it were going to hit me. I jumped out of the way. The BMW parked at the end of the driveway, and the driver went inside the house. The two teenagers laughed, and Lerato smiled at the "joke," revealing a black gap between his teeth.

While Lerato was speaking about why Luxolo was shot, his eyes darted around nervously. "They shoot you nowadays for anything," he said. "I heard it was over a mobile phone. They probably thought he took it." Lerato said that he had never known Luxolo to steal, and he didn't think he had done it. (Lerato might have meant that he didn't know Luxolo to steal from other black people, since he had a long history of stealing cars from white people.) I asked again if it could have been about something else. "He knows those guys from childhood," he said. "He must just think back to childhood, he must think."

He was fidgeting with a piece of seaweed, dried in the shape of a leafless tree that looked like the wind had blown all its branches east.

Lerato, who had known Luxolo for ten years, said that he was sorry about what happened. "I couldn't even look at him that day because of the blood," he said. "That night I felt terrible."

After the shooting, Lerato didn't call Nomsa, he said, because they had had a falling out the night before. She had come to the white gate looking for Luxolo, who hadn't been home in several days. Lerato and about thirty people were sitting on the lawn, listening to rap music and drinking. Nomsa grabbed the gate's metal bars, stared at Lerato and the crowd, then asked, "Where's my son?"

Lerato and the others at the party laughed at her. She started shaking the gate furiously and yelled, over and over, "You take all of Mandalay's children!" Nomsa wanted Lerato to open the gate so she could look for Luxolo, but he wouldn't. Instead, he replied, "Grow up—people come here of their own free will."

Later, back at her house, Mandisa was incensed by Lerato's account of what had transpired that night. She said it was clear that he was lying, and the only reason he took Luxolo to the hospital was to make sure that he didn't die on his lawn. He didn't call them out of guilt, she insisted.

"I think Lerato sent those people to shoot Luxolo," she said. "He knew what was going to happen."

Mandisa was especially angry with Lerato because she blamed him in part for the deterioration of her marriage. Before the shooting, she and Luxolo had broken up because he was spending so much time with Lerato:

> I told him every time *not* to go to that house. I asked him, *Can't you see what's happening? Lerato sleeps there with his girlfriend in their bed, and you sleep in Lerato's chair and play with his baby—not your own.* Everyone knows that house is bad and that everyone's children are there.

Mandisa and Luxolo had lived together for four years in the house that her mother had left her. In 2003, Mandisa's mother died of kidney disease, and her aunt came from the Eastern Cape Province to make funeral arrangements in accordance with Xhosa custom. Mandisa was nineteen and assumed that her aunt would be the executor of the estate until Mandisa turned twenty-one. Her mother's half-sister, who lived in Khayelitsha, told her that the aunt was trying to sell the house behind her back. Nomsa told Mandisa that they had to go to court to protect the estate. Mandisa, distraught over her mother's death, was grateful for Nomsa's guidance. At the courthouse, they ran into the aunt, who refused to greet them. The magistrate, a friend of Nomsa, looked at the will and said that everything had been left to Mandisa.

Her mother left her the house and about R120,000 ($20,000)—quadruple the average annual salary of an elementary school teacher. The funeral was to take place in the Eastern Cape, about an eight-hour drive from Cape Town. Nomsa, Luxolo, and Mandisa drove the whole day to Mandisa's grandmother's house for the funeral, but, once there, the family wouldn't let them in. Mandisa watched from the street as her mother's family ate and drank the food and alcohol paid for by her mother's estate. When the body was taken to the graveyard, the family also tried to stop them even from watching the burial, but they couldn't, since it was taking place on public property. That night Mandisa, Nomsa, and Luxolo drove home. Mandisa hasn't spoken to her mother's family since.

Nomsa, who had been a good friend of Mandisa's mother, suggested that Mandisa build four flats in the back of the house to rent. Mandisa did so and was thus able to support Luxolo and the baby with the money she earned. Meanwhile, Luxolo had difficulty keeping jobs. He quit his last job—working for Flexicell, selling discounted cell phone time—about three months before he was shot. "Sometimes he would have money, but I didn't know where he got it from," she said. She guessed it was from Nomsa, but she indicated that he never gave her any of it. Mandisa's mother had disliked Luxolo; before she died, she often told Mandisa that he was "no good."

For the first three years that they lived together, everything was fine, Mandisa said. The real problems started about a year ago, when she bought the white VW Golf with her mother's money. "I wanted him to get a job, support his baby and family," she said. "He'd take the car and come back after three days without calling." About a week before he was shot, the relationship had deteriorated to the point where she asked him to move out. "He wasn't home, he was drinking a lot," she said. "I had made a decision that I wanted to close the love in my heart."

He agreed without argument and took most of his things to his mother's house. "She was suffocating me," Luxolo explained. At times, Mandisa wondered whether he was staying with her only for the car. Though Nomsa knew and didn't approve of the fact that he wasn't working or spending time with his family, she felt that she was powerless to do anything about it. They both wished that he'd change.

Mandisa told Luxolo that he could have the car. She felt that the Golf had brought such bad things to their relationship that she didn't want it around. She said to him, "You go and do these crazy things with my mother's money, with my mother's house—it's bad luck." She explained, "in our culture it is believed that, with an inheritance, if you deal with it badly, it will come back to get you."

Before the shooting, Mandisa had a premonition. She was angry and told Nomsa that if anything happened to Luxolo, she and the baby wouldn't go to the funeral.

On December 16, she and Luxolo had a fight after he had stayed out with Lerato all night (on Luxolo's birthday). Mandisa decided that she needed a break and said that he would have to watch the baby while she and Nomsa went to visit an uncle in Khayelitsha. When she came back, later that night, the car was there, but the door to the house was locked. "I knocked

Mandisa watched from the street as her mother's family ate and drank the food and alcohol paid for by her mother's estate.

and knocked and knocked, and the baby woke and cried, and I thought he left the baby alone to go to that house," she said. Eventually, Nomsa and Mandisa broke the kitchen window to get to Sissy. They discovered Luxolo inside, curled up asleep on the bed. "He couldn't be *that* asleep from just alcohol," Mandisa said. Luxolo admitted that he had smoked *dagga* [marijuana], too. The next day, they didn't speak at all. Mandisa figured that he was out of her life for good. And then he was shot.

"I want him to walk," she confided in me. "If he doesn't, I have to stay with him. People will look at me so badly if I don't stay, even though I have valid reasons not to. If he could walk again, it would be easier to leave him."

• • •

ONE AFTERNOON MANDISA, Luxolo, and I were sitting outside when Nomsa arrived with good news. The police had arrested Ntsikelelo, and a hearing was scheduled for January 11, 2007. Ntsikelelo told the police that he wasn't at Lerato's house or with Bandile the night of the shooting. Ntsikelelo had been with another friend—whose name he couldn't remember and whose address he didn't know. Luxolo did not react; he was lying on the trolley and staring at the soft undulations of the gray-brown Boland Mountains. He was in a lot of pain, and Mandisa was massaging his back with white cream. People with spinal cord injuries often suffer from chronic and painful muscle spasms.

I asked Luxolo how he felt about the arrest, and he said that he didn't care, because he didn't think that Ntsikelelo would be punished. Justice in South Africa is elusive. The police and court systems, though better than in most African countries, are widely regarded as incompetent. The people that Mandisa knew who had committed crimes never spent a day in jail. For instance, she pointed out, Luxolo himself was arrested for car theft three times but was never convicted. "What's the point?" Mandisa lamented. "It will go on and on, and at the end we'll be where we started."

Nomsa, too, had become disillusioned with the new government, though she hadn't always been. Apartheid started when Nomsa was four years old. In 1976, she marched at the Soweto Riots, which marked the beginning of a strong resistance movement and apartheid's decline. "The police were shooting people like flies," Nomsa said, and she was right: approximately 500 people died. Several years later, Nomsa met Nelson Mandela, about whom she gushed, "I felt like I was meeting Jesus." She proudly voted in the first elections of 1994, but, as the years passed, she felt that one disastrous system had merely replaced another.

The police and court systems, though better than in most African countries, are widely regarded as incompetent.

"This government is corrupt," she said. "Unemployment and crime are worse now. At least under apartheid there was order. If you did something wrong, the police hanged you. Now no one is punished for anything." This sentiment is expressed by many South Africans, frustrated by rampant crime and violence.

Nomsa chose to pursue justice in her son's case, though she knew that the chances of conviction were slim. In many ways, it seemed she experienced his pain even more deeply than he did. While Luxolo didn't comprehend what the rest of his life might be like in a wheelchair, Nomsa did, and it devastated her. Making sure that Ntsikelelo was imprisoned was the only way she could feel at peace—she'd give the process all her strength.

As we sat outside, Nomsa reminisced about Luxolo as a baby:

Though Boetie is an old man now, I still remember the pain of giving birth. His head was so big, and it was a lot of stitches. Birth pain is a forgettable pain; it is when something happens to them that you remember.

On January 11, 2007, Nomsa, Mandisa, Senele, and I drove to the Mitchell's Plain courthouse at 8:45 AM. Nomsa arrived fifteen minutes early to ask the prosecutor to deny Ntsikelelo bail. The large brick building was crowded with hundreds of people sitting on benches or on the floor outside the various courtrooms. Luxolo had appeared in this same building when he was arrested and acquitted for stealing cars. In prosecutor Rochelle Haarmse's office, Nomsa fidgeted with her hands as she explained that Ntsikelelo had threatened her family: "We're scared that if he gets bail, he'll come for us," she said. Haarmse asked Nomsa to pick up the medical reports documenting Luxolo's condition from Groote Schuur Hospital. Officially, this was the responsibility of the police, but Haarmse said that the process would be much faster if she did it. Haarmse agreed to make an application to deny Ntsikelelo bail. "It's a pretty open-and-shut case," he indicated.

We sat down on the benches outside the courtroom. The first hearing was scheduled for 9:00 AM. It was 10:00 AM, and the magistrate hadn't arrived. Haarmse called Nomsa back into the office. Investigator Michael Nkenke, who had arrived a few minutes earlier, and Haarmse now said that they

Yesterday (2004), directed by Darrell James Roodt

would not make an application to deny bail. "There is not enough persuasive evidence of a direct threat," Haarmse said. The investigator added that Ntsikelelo was twenty-one, and his only priors were drunk driving and driving without a license. Nomsa didn't argue, but she was upset. She didn't understand what had changed since the earlier conversation. The investigator, she assumed, must have said something to Haarmse.

Back on the benches in the hallway, Nomsa thought that every older woman who passed might be Ntsikelelo's mother. The magistrate arrived at 10:30 AM, and as we sat inside the courtroom, Nomsa spotted Ntsikelelo's mother, sister, and girlfriend. They sat two rows behind us. A man in a light blue tracksuit walked a few rows in front of us and scanned the spectators until he saw Nomsa and Mandisa—he stared at them intently for a few seconds, making sure that they saw him. It was Bandile, the man whom Ntsikelelo said he did not know. Though Nomsa noticed him out of the corner of her eye, she did not look at him.

The magistrate looked no older than twenty-five and spoke softly, rarely looking up from the bench. The court clerk read the docket number, 3704247. A police officer escorted Ntsikelelo up a stairwell in the middle of the court.

The large brick building was crowded with hundreds of people sitting on benches or on the floor outside the various courtrooms. Ntsikelelo had a shaved head and sported white jeans and an orange velour sweatshirt that draped over his tall, lean body. He looked much smaller and younger than Luxolo. He stood before the magistrate with his shoulders slumped over. It was difficult to hear what the lawyers or magistrate were saying, except that Ntsikelelo was charged with attempted murder. Ntsikelelo's advocate read his client's not-guilty plea. He said that the defendant denied being at Lerato's house the night of the shooting. The advocate argued that Ntsikelelo should be released on nominal bail, on the grounds that he worked at an upscale restaurant, making 200 rand a week (about $30), and was taking a class in electrical engineering at a local college.

The prosecution didn't disagree, and the magistrate set bail at 500 rand (about $75 or two-and-a-half-week's pay). The magistrate set another court date for March 14, 2007. The hearing was finished, and Ntsikelelo turned and rushed down the stairs like a schoolboy late for class. He did not look at his family or Luxolo's—just fifteen feet away.

Sitting on the benches outside the courtroom, Nomsa and Mandisa were horrified. "How can you give someone 500 rand bail on attempted murder?!" Mandisa asked. "This was a total waste of time!" About twenty feet away sat Ntsikelelo's mother, wearing a straw sun hat and a light yellow blouse. She and her family looked relieved.

We left the courthouse. As we drove, Mandisa pointed to the Mitchell's Plain Day Hospital a few blocks away. "That's where Sissy was born," she

said, then paused for a moment, remembering, "That's where we found Luxolo after he was shot."

Yesterday (2004), directed by Darrell James Roodt

Nomsa drove to the mall. Senele was starting school in a week, and Nomsa needed to buy her uniform and supplies, which coincidentally cost about 500 rand. Mandisa looked at baby clothes for Sissy as she talked about a fight that she and Luxolo had had the night before. He wanted the 27-inch TV, which belonged to Mandisa, to be brought to him from the house. "No. It's not appropriate for this place," she said. "It's too big."

Luxolo shouted, "It's all about you and your things!"

She yelled back, "Yes, they are my things. I'm angry. I don't feel like doing things for you!" It was the first time she told him that she was angry since his injury. He became quiet. Nomsa, who was in the room, said she would try to borrow a TV from a friend. "She always gives in," Mandisa said. But Mandisa realized that if she didn't bring the TV, it would create more trouble for Nomsa, so she, too, finally gave in. Luxolo and Mandisa hadn't spoken since the fight, and she didn't visit him after the hearing. Nomsa did and told him what had happened. He didn't react.

On January 12, Mandisa and Nomsa took Sissy to visit Luxolo. Outside, Sissy stared at the strange apparatus that her father was lying on—the trolley intrigued her. Luxolo noticed her fascination and clutched her around the waist, lifting her to the side of the trolley, her chubby legs dangling over the edge. Mandisa gave the trolley a long push toward the wall, and Sissy broke into giggles as she glided across the courtyard. After Luxolo sat her down, she reached up and shook her arms, asking for another ride. Luxolo did it a few more times before becoming fatigued.

Mandisa said that it was time to go. She still wasn't speaking to Luxolo. Sissy gave her father a hug, and I walked them out. "He's still cross over the TV," Mandisa said. "I didn't even want to be here, but he wanted Sissy to come."

Luxolo wheeled himself to the cafeteria for dinner. The nurse placed a plate of spaghetti and green salad on his trolley. A red-haired nurse with a round tummy looked at Luxolo and said in Afrikaans, *"Waar is Lusanda?"*

"Don't worry—he'll come in a minute and make a big noise," Luxolo assured her.

Sure enough, Lusanda made a dramatic entrance, yelling—in Xhosa (a language she didn't understand)—about the "fat nurse." Lusanda was angry that she hadn't let him eat lunch in his room earlier that day. He parked himself next to Luxolo and talked about the progress he was making in physio. In the pool, he could take several steps by himself. Luxolo looked away. He had made no progress. He could still wiggle only three toes.

Outside, Sissy stared at the strange apparatus that her father was lying on—the trolley intrigued her.

After dinner, the nurses put Luxolo to bed next to Mandisa's 27-inch TV.

I asked what happened between them over the TV. "Mandisa picks a lot of fights," he said. "But I'm too down to talk to her now—I'm the one eating the dust." He wasn't concerned about whether Mandisa stayed with him; it was completely up to her, he said. But it wasn't. Mandisa wanted an apology. Mandisa wanted Luxolo to acknowledge that he had wronged her. Only then could she consider standing by him.

"I think it's best at a time like this to be alone," Luxolo said.

Luxolo told me that a couple of times before he was shot he went to the sea to speak with his ancestors, but he couldn't hear them clearly. They sounded angry, he said. Two nights after the hearing, Luxolo had another dream about the ocean:

> It was like I was in Khayelitsha, and there were trellises, but not with flowers—with roots, all tangled up. It was a big place, and I called this man over who had a dog with him—a dog in dreams is considered an ancestor. The man asked if I wanted to buy the dog, and I said, *No. It's an ugly dog, and it looks like a puppy.* There were two houses there, and they were also made of these roots, and there was this man putting out a fire who lived there. Then, I saw the sea. I asked this boy, *Is there a road to the sea?* and he said, *Yes.* So I walked down this road—it was in a valley—and when I came close to the sea, it was fighting and angry, and I was afraid. I moved closer, and every

time I lost the road—the sea covered it over. My baby was there, and she was going to fall into the ocean, and I picked her up with one hand, and she was heavy. I put her above me, and she was safe, and I walked closer to the sea. It started coming for me. The sea was going to swallow me. Then I woke up.

I asked Luxolo what he thought the dream meant. He said that maybe he was shot because his ancestors were angry with him. Maybe his lifestyle had insulted them; maybe he hadn't appreciated his blessings; maybe he had not spent enough time with his family. He paused, waved his hand dismissively, as the moment of introspection and humility vanished.

"All I know is I don't regret anything," he said. "What happened was how it was supposed to be, by the stars in the universe." ⊛

Yesterday (2004), directed by Darrell James Roodt

Yesterday

Nominated for the 2004 Academy Award for Best Foreign Language Film, *Yesterday*, directed by Darrell James Roodt, recounts the story of its eponymous heroine, a village woman in Zululand raising her young daughter, Beauty. The mother has been ill for several months, but the nearest clinic is far away and understaffed. Thanks to a taxi hired by a friend, Yesterday finally manages to arrive early enough to be able to see the doctor, who reveals that the cause of her persistent cough is none other than AIDS. Thus begins Yesterday's struggle over the course of a year to live her life as before, while knowing her imminent fate.

Yesterday travels to Johannesburg to speak with her husband—a miner away for months at a time—about her condition, which incites his denial and violent ire. Sometime later, he returns, gaunt and weak, to the village, at last ready to accept the truth, that he, too, has AIDS. Yesterday reminisces fondly of better days and cares lovingly for her husband, forgiving him for not only having brutally beaten but also having infected her. When a group of local women plot to take matters into their own hands (under the false belief that the disease can be "caught," like a common cold), Yesterday uses scrap metal to build a shelter-house where her husband can live out his last days in peace, away from the village.

The village sangoma advised Yesterday to release her pent-up anger, but not until her husband dies does that anger—clearly righteous—finally erupt, leading her to take a sledgehammer to the hospice she constructed with such care. Despite her deteriorating health, Yesterday maintains her dignity and experiences great joy in seeing her daughter off to her first day of school—a goal she set upon learning that she was terminally ill. Throughout the film, Yesterday shows how people can transcend the most adverse of conditions to lead worthy lives.

Yesterday is a visual meditation on life in a remote African village, offering a window onto the all-too-common plight of married African women, the group currently most threatened by AIDS. The film presents slow, pensive pans of quiet, undeveloped, and sparsely populated Zululand, connected to the modern world by long, dusty dirt roads over which an invisible urban enemy travels to strike victims far removed from the city in every other way.

Yesterday (2004), directed by Darrell James Roodt

Urgent Tasks for African Scholars in the Humanities

Moradewun Adejunmobi

HOW SHOULD AFRICAN scholars in the humanities respond to the wave of autochthony-inspired movements sweeping across the African continent, which has already received considerable attention from social scientists in specialized publications? Does any part of the work that we do directly address this and other challenges confronting Africa in the early twenty-first century? As scholars, we must keep pace with scholarship and debates in the world at large. But how frequently do we really bring humanistic scholarship to bear on pressing matters in contention in our societies of origin? How frequently do we scholars in the humanities make the polemics unfolding in contemporary Africa the focus of our work?

In speaking of the promotion of autochthony as one example of a current African crisis, I refer here to conflicts such as the wars in the Congo and Côte d'Ivoire [the Ivory Coast], the Rwandan genocide, and the unfolding crisis in Darfur that has spilled over into Chad. I refer also to the rising tide of xenophobia in South Africa, which sadly has erupted into scattered attacks against African immigrants around the country. In addition, there are many less-well-publicized conflicts all over the continent between diverse *indigenes*—a term now widely used in Africa, especially in English-speaking West Africa, to refer to individuals who claim roots in a particular location—and settlers, between farmers and either herders or so-called hunter-gatherers.

Social scientists have advanced a number of proposals to explain the current appeal of autochthony in Africa. Some attribute its growing popularity to developments in democratization and decentralization, which require communities to determine which individuals count as legitimate *citizens*, that is, those entitled to vote in a given territory. Colonial preferences for migration and World Bank policies that encourage communities to bypass the state have also played a role in bringing about the current state of affairs. According to some scholars, renewed dependence on extractive resources has made control of territory with desired resources imperative for those who want to exercise power and gain wealth. In yet other cases, environmental degradation pits communities that once lived in relative harmony against one another in a bid to control shrinking plots of

fertile land. Those who work on globalization tend to interpret the intensi-
fication of ethnic mobilization around the world as one of many by-products
associated with globalization.

In addition to all of these factors, Africans today, and especially the
poor who make up the majority, are living through and confronting an
unparalleled sense of insecurity about physical space. Whether they live in
the city or in a rural area, many Africans cannot be certain that they will
have the right tomorrow to call "home" the place that they call it today.
Declining economies drive neighbors, friends, and even siblings to desperate battles over landed property and territory. Given the weak institutions
of their states, individuals can so easily be dispossessed of their property
that both young and old may be consumed with a desire to emigrate.
However, even when such Africans succeed in fleeing their homeland, they
often have to endure harassment and worse, inflicted by self-described
"indigenes" in their new place of residence.

Clearly, distinctions between "early" indigenes and "later" settlers are
not new in Africa, though the political currency of "indigenousness" has
lately acquired new value. In contemporary times, the very institutions of
the State have taken on the task not only of deter-
mining who arrived first but also of instigating
confrontations between so-called immigrants and
indigenes. Such was the case in Côte d'Ivoire, a
country whose recent experience reveals the limitations of currently fashionable celebrations of
cosmopolitanism, on the one hand, and older cri-
tiques of nativism, on the other. I am thinking in particular of the work of
such notable African humanists as F. Abiola Irele, in his famous 1987 lecture
"In Praise of Alienation"; or Kwame Anthony Appiah's more recently articulated positions on cultural contamination and cosmopolitanism, in his 2006
book, *Cosmopolitanism*.

> **Many Africans cannot be certain that they will have the right tomorrow to call "home" the place that they call it today.**

• • •

A BRIEF HISTORY of the Ivorian crisis is in order. Following the death in 1993
of Félix Houphouët-Boigny, the country's founding president, a struggle
broke out among the leading contenders for succession. To consolidate his
claims, the southern heir apparent Henri Konan Bédié invoked the principle
of *Ivoirité* against the northern Prime Minister, Alassane Ouattara, whose
parents were born in what is now Burkina Faso. Though Bédié initially
seemed to win the battle for succession, his hold on power remained tenu-
ous, and he was overthrown in a coup by Robert Guéï in 1999. Guéï promised to organize elections in 2000, and he, too, invoked the principle of
Ivoirité in order to exclude Ouattara. Despite his attempts to rig the

Jems Robert Koko Bi, *Les Enfants de Gorée.* 2000. Burnt poplar wood, 34 × 300 × 300 cm. ©2009 Artists Rights Society (ARS), New York / VG Bild-Kunst, Bonn

elections, Guëï lost to a long-time opponent of Houphouët, Laurent Gbagbo, who also used *Ivoirité* to reinforce his own popularity and to exclude Ouattara's mainly northern and Dyula-speaking supporters. Following the election debacle, Guëï withdrew to the countryside, accompanied by some disgruntled soldiers.

In 2002, an attempted coup split the army into pro-northern and pro-southern camps, marking the beginning of a civil war. The country was effectively partitioned, with the north being controlled by those whose citizenship had been questioned, and the south by the partisans of *Ivoirité*. To de-escalate tensions, a contingent of the French army occupied a line of demarcation between the north and south. This provoked the anger of the Jeunes Patriotes [Young Patriots], a group of youths active in southern cities who took to harassing, expelling, and even killing not only immigrants but also Ivorians from the north of the country, whose citizenship they denied. Acts of violence against civilians were also reported on the northern side of the line of demarcation. Successive efforts by various African heads of state to bring the war to an end failed until March 2007, when the latest of many peace agreements was signed, followed by a ceremony in July 2007 to mark the end of hostilities.

It is specifically in the light of recent manifestations of the politics of autochthony in places such as Côte d'Ivoire that I would like to revisit the implications of the now-popular praise of cultural alienation—or advocacy on behalf of cosmopolitanism—among African scholars in the humanities. Broadly speaking, I embrace the spirit of openness to other cultures that informs African scholars such as Irele and Appiah in their writings on the cultural politics of post-independence Africa, on the one hand, and globalization, on the other. But I also believe that the call for alienation in response to the cultural nationalism of the 1980s has, in the early twenty-first century, been overshadowed by events on the ground.

A reasoned praise of alienation and contamination undoubtedly served as a rebuttal to the advocacy of nativism, and also contributed to ongoing debates about the place of indigenous culture in societies transformed by the colonial encounter. But this particular debate, which was timely in the 1980s, does not quite get to the root of the crisis currently confronting many African communities. The framework required for these times is one that directly addresses the politics of autochthony, belonging, and indigenousness, not so much of cultures, but of peoples. To be relevant, the new framework must confront the question of what it means to *belong* to a territory.

Informed observers may ask: *Isn't the Ivorian experience an example of nativism run amok? Wouldn't the architects of* Ivoirité *have benefited from a significant dose of alienation and greater openness to other cultures?* But such questions reflect a misdiagnosis of the problem. One of the most interesting dimensions of the politics of autochthony in contemporary Africa is that its most virulent advocates have hardly ever been cultural nationalists seeking cultural purity. If Bédié occasionally dabbled in the politics of cultural nationalism, the same cannot be said for Gbagbo or Guéï or, more importantly, for the hundreds of young men who make up the Jeunes Patriotes. In the same breath that members of the Jeunes Patriotes excoriated the French for supposedly intervening on the side of the northern rebels, they called for U.S. intervention in Côte d'Ivoire. In any case, most of the aggression was directed against other Africans, and usually other Ivorians, not Europeans. In other words, the *least* foreign of the so-called foreigners bore the brunt of the violence.

Openness toward "foreign" cultures in postcolonial Africa has often been more a question of consumption than of conviction.

Some observers have described Gbagbo as more of an anti-imperialist who managed to rally an ideologically disparate movement of youth equally opposed to West African immigrants, French interests in Côte d'Ivoire, and the international financial institutions that had imposed unpopular policies on the country. *Ivoirité* as defined by Gbagbo bore only minimal resemblance to Mobutu's *authenticité*: there was no systematic program of cultural reform; there were no name changes or revised fashion codes. Indeed, Gbagbo continued to appear at public and international events in his well-tailored European suits, even as he castigated European powers, especially the French. And whatever emblems of *Ivoirité* Gbagbo introduced to his youthful followers were more likely to be presented as signs of a newly minted Ivorian identity than as relics from the distant past.

In this regard, the Ivorian situation is fairly typical of contemporary Africa. Notwithstanding the upsurge of conflicts over territory and increased incidence of ethnic mobilization, cultural nationalism, as such, actually seems to be on the wane, particularly among the youth. If anything, today's African youth, even at their most xenophobic, appear distrustful of

Jems Robert Koko Bi, *Entre deux troncs.* 2001. Oak wood, 250 x 80 x 75 cm. ©2009 Artists Rights Society (ARS), New York / VG Bild-Kunst, Bonn

tradition, and culturally ecumenical. But then, as many Africanists have noted, openness toward "foreign" cultures in postcolonial Africa has often been more a question of consumption than of conviction. A willingness to adopt the latest Western youth fashions, for example, does not necessarily signify acceptance of the principles that regulate social or political life in Western societies.

• • •

I WOULD ARGUE that the politics of autochthony and the bloodletting associated with it are not in fact founded on an ideology of nativism. Rather, this tragic turn in the social behavior of African communities derives from a growing sense of insecurity about the spaces in which people reside and work. Many such spaces are still designated as places of origin, but can no longer deliver the benefits expected of a home, or a space where one can reside and work without fear. In a situation of stagnant and failing economies, along with demographic pressures on fertile land exacerbated by political uncertainty, many individuals, especially the youth, experience a feeling of being adrift in the world.

Purging territory designated as *home* of outsiders appears to be the most decisive and only accessible expression of power available to people in desperate conditions seeking to regain control over their lives and the spaces they inhabit. The violence unleashed on defenseless neighbors is not necessarily about recovering indigenous traditions; it may be, instead, about regaining control over self and space. Indeed, the youth enrolled in various militias and armies around Africa have shown themselves perfectly capable of disrespecting their elders and trampling upon tradition. And, if asked to sample or even adopt foreign cultures, today's African youth may do so happily, though this act need not prevent them from killing their neighbors, if those

The most violent confrontations in Africa are battles over foreign bodies in local *territory*.

neighbors happen to be designated as "foreigners," or "outsiders," competing with indigenes for scarce resources. The most violent confrontations in Africa at this time are, first and foremost, battles over foreign bodies in local *territory*, not battles over foreign culture as such. The triggers for this violence, namely, the hankering for a home that functions as such, should be not dismissed but taken seriously. A critique of nativism and essentialism in African cultural politics does not provide a satisfactory way out of this war over territory, nor can it. But that is not to say that discussions about culture and the humanities writ large are entirely irrelevant to the problem at hand.

Ultimately, the way to bring these wars over territory to an end is for all interested parties, including intellectuals and policy makers within and outside Africa, to engage very deliberately with the concept of *territoriality*, and what it might mean for contemporary Africa, in the face of dwindling resources, deteriorating ecologies, and fragile economies. This means addressing a variety of questions and policy issues, including those that pertain to the political demarcation of territory and land tenure practices; the political representation of citizens and noncitizens; the process of migration within and outside political boundaries; control over resources contained within a territory; and the sustainability of lifestyles, both of so-called indigenes and so-called settlers.

We cannot, I believe, understand the current appeal of autochthony, nor stamp it out, without first coming to terms with the centrality of territoriality in current conflicts over identity in Africa.

· · ·

SKEPTICS MAY WONDER whether one can prevent any discussion of territoriality from degenerating into a discourse of nativism, particularly in the hands of unprincipled politicians, who will do whatever their conscience—or lack thereof—allows them to do, in order to get elected. One both hopes and presumes that a substantial proportion of African intellectuals and scholars will be less bound by the exigencies of such short-term priorities. But, at this point in time, the work of such intellectuals will be of minimal usefulness, if it fails to directly address the looming crisis over questions of territoriality. It is not enough simply to reject the politics of autochthony; African intellectuals must also be willing to explore alternative means for understanding territory and identity.

Over the past two decades, the tendency among scholars of postcolonialism has been to throw the baby out with the bathwater whenever discussion has turned to exclusive and violent constructions of identity. We have been more preoccupied with deconstructing nativism and nationalism than with seriously investigating the possibility of promoting alternative and safer forms of territorialized identity. But the problems of autochthony in contemporary Africa cannot be resolved by celebrating mobility or summarily dismissing the current obsession with territoriality. Indeed, we already have a mobile population that is at the same time engrossed with claiming territory. And, in all likelihood, the conditions under which much of this mobility occurs may be intensifying the compulsion to claim territory in situations where neither "hosts" nor "migrants" can find a place to pursue sustainable lifestyles without fear of expulsion.

What the African foot soldiers of autochthony seek is a place where they can live, work, and realize their public and private aspirations in relative safety.

The challenge for African intellectuals and policy makers today is to propose productive ways of engaging with territoriality that do not involve embracing xenophobia, ethnic cleansing, and racism, etc. There must be a concerted effort to reclaim current practices of territoriality from diverse demagogues, and this effort I propose as a new *ethics of locality*. What the African foot soldiers of autochthony seek is a place where they can live, work, and realize their public and private aspirations in relative safety. To the extent that African intellectuals and policy makers are able to propose and popularize practical mechanisms for achieving these goals without making a detour through ideologies of exclusion, to that degree,

they will have contributed to stemming the violence generated by the politics of autochthony.

Localities exist as such for individuals in relation to the scope and boundaries of the territory where they and the communities with which they identify are currently situated. I prefer the term *locality* to *territory*, since *territory* is often associated with political jurisdiction, with the presumption in many cases that loyalty to one politically demarcated territory might be incompatible with commitment to the interests of other politically demarcated territories.

Distinctions between the exercise of political authority over activities in a territory and an ethical practice of locality are especially critical in Africa, given the abuses of political power to which many African communities have been subjected. It was, after all, Ivorian government officials who, in 2006, at the height of the hysteria over *Ivoirité*, gave permission to a ship owned by a Dutch company to dump over 400 metric tons of toxic waste in Abidjan, the capital of *Ivoirité*. More than 70,000 people fell ill, and at least ten people died. But political leaders are not the only ones guilty of disregarding locality. As economic conditions have worsened, self-gratification at the expense of locality has become a way of life for African youth, with the difference that their acts of self-gratification more consistently and directly involve gratuitous violence than do those of older politicians. In short, while an ethical practice of locality might overlap with a recognition of political boundaries, it often involves more than a manipulation of political jurisdiction for either personal or ideological gain. A broad-based solidarity with the diverse constituencies that comprise the local community is also essential.

Jems Robert Koko Bi, *Têtes.* 2006. Platan wood, 90 x 70 x 300 cm. ©2009 Artists Rights Society (ARS), New York / VG Bild-Kunst, Bonn

• • •

IF THE WAR in Côte d'Ivoire has truly come to an end, Ivorians will have to learn to live together again. However, rebuilding trust among variously designated citizens and immigrants, as well as indigenes and settlers, is sure to be more difficult than simply signing a treaty in Ouagadougou and lighting a flame in Bouaké. A new vision of what it means to be Ivorian will have to be fostered by developing policies that directly confront prevailing concerns over territoriality and citizenship, and by transmitting the principles undergirding such policies to Ivorian youth through the educational system. In this regard, the universities, too, have a role to play.

What is remarkable and tragic about the Ivorian case is how easily scholars who had been opponents of Houphouët-Boigny for decades fell under the sway of the politics of autochthony, once their primary adversary disappeared from the political stage. It is certainly possible that some activist intellectuals "sold themselves to the highest bidder," so to speak, after the contest to succeed Houphouët began, but more worrisome is that the majority of intellectual collaborators with Houphouët's successors seem to have been true believers in the cause of autochthony. Their criticism of Houphouët's tendency to promote immigrants and foreigners to positions of authority evidences the ease with which they embraced autochthony. Be that as it may, many of Houphouët's opponents found no better ideology to commend to Ivorians in the wake of Houphouët's death than one founded on the politics of autochthony.

Scientific study will not effect significant transformations in a community where major constituencies in the community have yet to rethink community goals and lifestyles.

The word *Ivoirité* itself may have been first invented by Niangoranh Porquet, a playwright and scholar, in the 1970s. Houphouët's successors appropriated and extended the concept, while calling upon like-minded scholars to provide intellectual support for the political project of *Ivoirité*, which consisted in reclaiming Ivorian independence by expelling those designated as "foreigners" from the country. Professors in the humanities, particularly those in literature and history, played a prominent role in developing intellectual rationalizations for *Ivoirité*.

For example, Gbagbo, who had been not only an activist, but also a historian of long standing, used his own research, and his well-established ties with the largest Ivorian student organizations, to further promote the idea of *Ivoirité*. Unable to rely on a unified army for support, Gbagbo made the youth his power base. That the idea of autochthony should have had such an appeal for Ivorian youth, including educated youth, is, perhaps, unsurprising. They were aware that, under prevailing conditions, there would be no fulfillment of the lofty aspirations acquired through their education and from the media. The apostles of *Ivoirité* offered clearly accessible means for supposedly attaining desired goals. With few other alternatives at hand, groups of Ivorian youth seized upon the tools that they had been given by their intellectual mentors.

Scholars who became spokespersons for *Ivoirité* were definitely putting the humanities to public use, which was, in itself, commendable. Anywhere in the world, and particularly in those places where conditions of life are challenging, humanistic study should have a public dimension. But, contrary to popular belief among African politicians and even many intellectuals, scientific study alone, divorced from a larger cultural context, cannot transform African communities. Investments in new technologies and scientific study will not effect significant transformations in a community where major constituencies in the community have yet to rethink community goals and lifestyles. Ultimately, the critical decisions that transform communities are made by human beings, not by machines. But the many—or few—who have access to intermediate and higher education in Africa will hardly be equipped to contribute constructively to a reorientation of their communities without a more general rethinking of the role and content of the humanities in the educational system.

Studying the humanities could and should provide a forum through which African students and teachers alike may begin to question and redefine the world in which they live. The humanities offer the best opportunity within the school system for teaching critical thinking skills and instilling self-confidence, as well as encouraging creativity and inventiveness. But African humanities scholars must also engage with the pressing questions of the moment, including the rise of autochthony-inspired movements. A review of humanistic study in the universities should thus be one of the many elements deployed, especially

Instead of simply taking the categories for granted, the categories themselves can become the springboard for examining what it means to belong to the location, to the nationality, to the ethnic group, etc.

in a country like Côte d'Ivoire, where educated youth and scholars in the humanities have played such a prominent role in advocating and implementing the politics of autochthony. Humanistic study can serve this function, given its focus on ethnicity, nationality, locality, gender, race, and related classifications. But instead of simply taking the categories for granted, the categories themselves can become the springboard for examining what it means to belong to the location, to the nationality, to the ethnic group, etc. Communities frequently use their cultural practices to transform indistinct places into identifiable homes. Yet there is no reason why any locality should be associated with a monolithic culture. And where better to begin questioning the spatialization of singular cultures and singular identities than in the humanities?

Jems Robert Koko Bi, *Innen*. 1999. Poplar wood, 190 × 80 × 65 cm. ©2009 Artists Rights Society (ARS), New York / VG Bild-Kunst, Bonn

What does it mean to be Ivorian if the best-known writer from the country, Ahmadou Kourouma, is a northerner? What new approaches might be used in teaching Kourouma's *Soleils des indépendances* (1968) or Jean-Marie Adiaffi's *La Carte d'identité* (1980) in Ivorian schools and elsewhere in Africa, in the light of the recent conflicts over border-crossing, immigration, and indigenousness? Ivorian urban popular culture offers even more opportunity for examining these questions. Should the reggae music produced by performers such as Alpha Blondy and Tiken Jah Fakoly be considered Ivorian, when these artists are Dyula-speaking individuals who hail from the north of the country? Is the music of one of the most successful southern music bands, Magic System, to be considered Ivorian though the members often sing in French—Ivorian French, admittedly, but French all the same? And if Ivorian French mixed with other Ivorian languages is considered more Ivorian than French, then what is it that prevents individuals whose mother tongues have been spoken for centuries on the territory of what is now Côte d'Ivoire from claiming membership in communities within that politically defined territory? It is precisely because

African popular culture lends itself to these kinds of questions that civics lessons for the youth in contemporary Africa should include a serious examination of the forms of popular culture that are either locally produced or locally consumed.

Clearly, the educational system must also acquaint young people with the indigenous cultures of their locality. But, in contemporary Africa, it may be more productive to approach all societies and all cultures from the perspective of interactions with neighboring groups rather than from the standpoint of a fixed indigeneity. Ivorian students need to know, for example, how Ivorian ethnic groups such as the Baule, Bété, and Dyula have migrated and interacted with one another over the past several centuries.

It will not be enough simply to criticize the advocates of autochthony, or even the nativists. It will not be enough to call on Africans to embrace Western intellectual traditions—or Asian ones, for that matter, now that increased attention is being focused on the economic prowess of India and China. The ravages caused by the politics of autochthony call for urgent intervention from African scholars in all fields, especially the humanities. African intellectuals who are dissatisfied with the politics of autochthony will need to propose an alternative paradigm for resolving the crisis over matters of belonging and territoriality, one that moves beyond both recommending cultural cosmopolitanism and mobility, and castigating nativism. At least some of our conversation in scholarly conferences and publications should explore practical responses to the diverse crises and challenges currently confronting African societies. It is in this spirit that I propose a new *ethics of locality* as a potentially fruitful subject of discussion by African scholars in the humanities. All of our work need not be driven by the crisis *du jour*. But there is a sense in which we must regain a rigorous and balanced practice of public relevance, which seems to have eluded us in recent years. Even more than advocacy on behalf of alienation, which we have continued to reiterate while disregarding new challenges, the example of public relevance, then, may be the most important lesson of Irele's "In Praise of Alienation."

Jems Robert Koko Bi

As an artist who was born and raised in the Ivory Coast but now lives in Germany, Jems Robert Koko Bi is struck on a nearly daily basis by the importance of space and history. Space marks the place where the artist lives and works; history follows him like a shadow. The contact between space and history is often strife-ridden, and these two facets of reality can be especially difficult to reconcile for an African artist living in the West.

Jems Robert Koko Bi has been inspired by his experience of confrontations between space and history to create sculptures out of wood, a material found in the complex and dynamic natural world. Yet wood retains through the creative process a neutrality that permits the expression of conflict without introducing even more. Because space and history, while in conflict, are integral parts of the artist's self, he has infused both in his works in wood, a medium which, he explains, "frees the spirit, makes it possible to play with multiple forms that highlight both plenitude and emptiness, the positive and the negative, contrasts which, in turn, give rise to countless new potential avenues for thought."

Through sculpting wood, the artist affirms his identity while enjoying an infinite sense of liberty. But Koko Bi regards himself as not changing the world but representing what he finds in it: the magnificent when it is magnificent, the deplorable when it is deplorable. He has burned some of his works, in a collaborative process through which the beauty and independence of the medium itself are affirmed, thus revealing the partnership between the artist and the wood.

I have always been searching for a way to say "No." But "No" to what exactly, I have never fully understood, nor how to comprehend the motives behind this inclination. I wanted to say "No" to the idea that an African child must follow the dictates of his father. I wanted to say "No" to corruption. But I also wanted to say "No" to myself, and to difficulties that were not difficult enough.

—Jems Robert Koko Bi

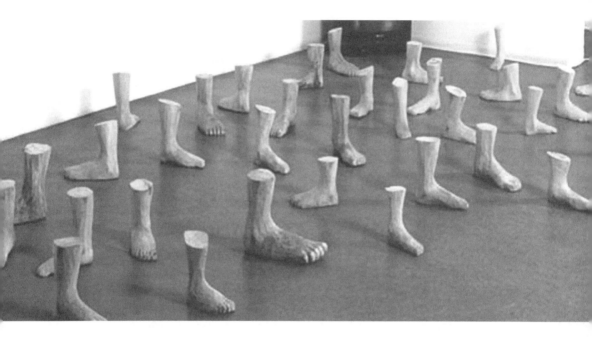

Jems Robert Koko Bi, *Témoins*. 2000. Poplar wood, 34 x 24 x 400 cm.

From the Notebooks of Antioch Sy

an excerpt

Miranda Pyne

Monsieur Couché, I am looking at your comments, the red scrawl with which you have defaced my essay. This low grade of D is undeserved.

Name: Antioch Sy

Subject: Philosophy

Antioch: The task was to write about a criminal act. While this is another interesting attempt to tell me the story of your unusual situation, I can't accept it. You have provided me with a long, rambling, semi-autobiographical, pornographic, and biased piece of writing. There are many problems with your writing, too. Your long sentence structure is strange in places; split infinitives remain a problem. This will not do. Please see me after class.

Really, *Monsieur Couché! Why do you need so much convincing?*

My father, Amadou Sy, did *eventually return home with wife number five. And* she did *try to do him in with one of those roadside African poisons. His intestines* did *twist up—part of those organs were surgically removed—and all this on top of the cancer. He is recovering, even if in mourning about his new young bride who betrayed him so unexpectedly. There is no* semi *to it. It is* true. *It is hard to make sense of it. I'm sorry it is indelicate. I am glad that I'm his daughter and not one of his wives.*

I should tell you, Monsieur Couché, that there is a young American woman, Alexandra Dufus, who has come to our home to do research on us. She says that she originally won a grant to interview young people, but then she met Arielle (my father's fourth wife), and, in getting to know her, she discovered that my old man is a polygamist. Now she wants to study us and turn us into a book. This Alex, she is cool—to an extent. Yesterday she asked me what young girls like me do for fun in such an exciting city as Paris. In your opinion, knowing me as your student, Monsieur Couché, do you think she is asking the right person?

I am determined to write something. In any case, you request that I do a rewrite because you find all my papers inappropriate. I may give it to Alexandra Dufus; I may give it to you; I may just keep it for myself and add it to all my other notes that I am working on to create a long graphic novel, you know, the one we talked about before, which is going to be all about my missing mother, and my future, and moving beyond Amadou Sy's constant betrayal. My best friend, Charlotte, always asks me What has been the extent of your dad's betrayal? *meaning something like* When will I stop being angry? *I don't know.*

I think I am a well-liked young woman. I am of few words and many thoughts, though I don't have much time alone to think. That must have some part to play in my frustration. I have been told that I am a fantasist. My head is full of fantasies that swirl above my reality. But the reality is that I live in a congested urban arrondissement *in Paris—the Paris of Africans and mice, the smelly Paris that Sarkozy might like to wash away.*

Boulevard du Temple, where we live, is one of a few streets bounded by ethnic cafés, populated by little shops where customers barter and old women smell fruit. Our apartment building is hidden between a florist and a new, ugly huddle of houses, near a small ancient triangle of green, where lonely people sit in the afternoons and wonder how they can bear their existence, and where, on Fridays, families of boys, dressed in shabby, silvery grey, congregate after prayers at the Rue Depestre Mosque. Our building, number 23, is a matter of upstairs and down, with thin corrugated-steel banisters and balconies bound by tulip-shaped railings. It is the scrawl in the right corner of the creaky lift, and the brightly blue-tiled courtyard; it is the seven-foot green plants in terracotta vessels, and the wooden shelves for foreign mail vulnerable to rifling neighbors.

I share this apartment of six rooms with my father, Amadou Sy, and his three wives and three siblings. As I told you, wife number five vanished with her hundred suitcases. Back to Africa, we think, but she could be anywhere: London, Romania. Nobody is looking for her. My father is not supposed to have four wives here, anyway. I don't fault her entirely. Her contempt for us spanned the neighborhood. Madame Sylvie called her "illiterate" every day. What is worse, she had no rebuttal. You have to learn to think fast in our house—otherwise, you will die. When those women fight, it is like barrels of thunder, ripostes that will strike you dead right there, tears that break your heart. My own mother, Zahara—she was my father's third wife—was the only one to get a divorce. That was nine years ago, when I was ten. She left us all for New York, where she opened her own hairdresser shop and sings with a band every so often. Mohammed, an older brother, and Mariam and shy Kanaté, two younger sisters, live here, too. I have older siblings, but they no longer live in Paris.

The interior of the apartment is very different from the neighborhood in which it is situated. It is a private building of apartments owned by the city of Paris and distributed by select people to selected people. There's been a tradition of blacks in this building. Nadja Hakimi, a widow, and her son Hamid live downstairs. An ex-Kenyan ambassador and his Italian wife are in apartment two. In 1962, some tolerant Frenchman decided to rent our apartment to a wealthy Senegalese family, who then passed it on to an oil-rich Malagasy man who owned half of Antananarivo. A flamboyant politician from Guadeloupe then rented it to us for the duration of my father's UN posting. We will have to give it back to him one day, as will he to its original owners.

We are fortunate, even though truly cash poor, to live here, a bit like bourgeoisie fallen from grace. Inside, the space is big, almost grand and elegant: the floorboards smell of vanilla, fragrant from the numerous aromatic wooden sculptures left behind by the Malagasy tenants. The furniture is threadbare, and it remains this way, as we cannot afford to re-upholster them. Turkish rugs left behind are strewn everywhere. They run the length of the corridor, crumpling up when the kids play vigorously, and their corners have tripped blind Fatou too many times to count. They are worn thin from the constant treading of people, for this is an apartment that has welcomed travelers who in return have bequeathed us their trinkets and heavy furniture, people whose lives are etched into the walls. This place is old, and ever since wife number five tried to hurt my father, we inhabit it like new-born ghosts, frightened of ourselves. The apartment is littered with newspapers, some of them twenty years old. My mothers use them to mop up spillages, and Arielle saves random recipes that she never makes. White typing paper is piled, rolled, and jammed behind things. It is lodged in corners under wooden shelves because my father and Madame Sylvie write, and my sisters like nothing more than to color and draw. My father has a fantasy that we can reuse every scrap from the printer.

Despite all the women in the household, despite the woman who comes once a week to clean, everywhere here there is visible dust. It covers the leaves of healthy blooming plants that hang from doorways; it sits on black lacquer tables and on blood red Chinese stools that align the eye with paintings on the walls. One of the paintings belongs to me: a portrait of my mother, an African beauty with inscrutable, youthful eyes. Her wild, bushy hair is tamed into a plait that snakes past a thin silk shoulder strap. At the bottom of the picture is an indelible black biro scrawl in someone's small childish handwriting, probably mine: I hate Momo! *Poor Momo, he is now my favorite brother, a twenty-nine-year-old who acts like he is seventeen.*

In general, I'd say we struggle financially. Our salary diminishes as the family grows. Not only are there the kids in the house to pay for, but my father must shell out money for my older sister, Aissatou, in dental school in Poland, and Jacques, his eldest son, who is training to be a doctor in America. My father is always giving out money, reminding us that he pays for water, for toothpaste, for my cigarettes. I just laugh when he says that, thinking, You should have thought of that before marrying the whole of Africa! *Then I leave the faucet on for five seconds longer than I would have ordinarily.*

. . .

To AN OLDER generation of Senegalese, we at 23 Boulevard du Temple appear a good family that follows the old ways. The men who can afford it still keep the Allah-granted quota of four wives. Amadou Sy's French-born children are clean and educated; none of us are delinquents. How can it be that of my father's wives who remain with him, all are seemingly dutiful. Madame Sylvie and her sister Fatou have lived in France for over fifty years, more time than they spent in their parents' village in Senegal. Arielle is no better. She was born here but traded in her progressive, Gabonese father and her Martiniquais mother for my father's system. Still, in our small ways, we resist the time warp of my father's own making. My family is numerous, pressed against each other. We are pulled about in ideology. We pretend to believe in my father's way, but in order to survive we have come to believe and to do otherwise.

When my parents' friends come to visit, they must wonder. And once they get over the fact that my father is a polygamist and that two of his wives are sisters, they must pour scorn on our heads: Those poor women. *In Africa, each of my father's wives might have had her own house by now. Here, they live crowded together. Each wife is no longer divine, an oracle in my father's ear; she has been doubly stripped, and, with the exception of Arielle—who works as a health worker at a women's internment center—each is in her old age financially dependent on my father. Actually, I don't know who is more dependent on whom.*

Madame Sylvie is the matriarch of this place, the ship's captain. She is my father's senior wife, and she is the fattest. She is in her seventies. Her face is thin, her body fat. There is no fruit shape that describes her. Senior wife? *I've studied the privileges for years, and this label means that she gets first dibs on everything. Now, in her late seventies, she enjoys a white Mercedes, and in the bathroom everything from bidet to bath salts is in indigo and cream. But there is no diet pill or cream that seems to work for her.*

Madame Sylvie has done an okay job with the pittance my father expects the rest of us to share for bills, school fees, doctors' bills, clothes, and food. She has decorated the common spaces with indigo baskets and traditional cloth, and it is not her fault that we are not, as far as I can see, gaining or acquiring anything of importance. She has prevented the very foul habit that some old men have of spitting their kola nuts on the floor, and that has kept the floors relatively clean.

In the pecking order, Madame Sylvie is followed by her sister Fatou. Fatou is the prettiest woman in the neighborhood, but she will never know. She lost her eyesight from a river parasite when she was just a girl. Adjusting to her new condition in the village, she developed a limp. The story goes that my father, urged on by her younger sister Sylvie, married Fatou out of pity, because the blind fend for themselves in the village of her birth. It is true that Madame Sylvie was lonely in Paris. But it is false that Fatou believes that she could never have fended for herself. My father must have mused helplessly over what was once Fatou's hourglass waist, her sweet, upward-turning lips, her strong nose and hollow cheeks. He needed no persuading, no entreaties from her concerned sister. He probably realized in a lightening flash that it was not such a bad proposition to take on such a woman, even though disabled. Madame Sylvie had trouble conceiving, so it was a good arrangement when she became a devoted mother to Fatou's four children, loving them so dearly, even as much as her own son, Mohammed, born many years later. My father had no trouble courting blind Fatou, too, with wilting flowers and food—as he always does—until she became overweight.

Arielle, the indéfatigable Arielle, as our Kenyan neighbor calls her, follows Fatou. She arrived during my mother's watch, when I was only three. Though she is not as smart as Madame Sylvie, and a lot of junk comes out of her mouth, Arielle engages with my father on an intellectual level far more than the others do. Into the chaos of those early days, he brought in Arielle, younger than Zahara, an unstable woman, turbaned and twitchy, dragged down by a library of issues.

The last six months have taken their toll on Arielle. First, at her job at a refugee center, she listens all day long to stories of women who have lost everything and who are waiting in constant dread of deportation. These women—from Africa, Afghanistan, Eastern Europe, Iraq—relay sorrows that are beyond her comprehension. She tells us how they quell pain by cutting their arms and tender out-of-sight places on their bodies. They tell her that they can't sleep, don't trust their doctors or the other women whose rooms they share, and that it is terrifying for them to follow rules they don't understand. These women understand what it means to be poor, to live like a refugee, but they cannot comprehend why France has made them into prisoners. Their minds hurt. When Arielle returns home, she says her mind hurts, too, all the time. She tells us gruesome stories every night. At first we listened to them, but then it began to seem as if those sullen outsiders were sitting at our table alongside us, or ever present, hidden among my father's last wife's one hundred suitcases.

Arielle rages about the plight of the Senegalese men who are leaving their fishing villages to come to Europe in small fishing boats. She watches, aghast, when the patrol boats, planes, and helicopters from Spain and Italy buzz around all those twisted black bodies littering sandy beaches. She is enraged for those who get as far as the shore, alive, and then are turned back. She cries when she hears about their wooden pirogues that capsized. She cries about people losing their livelihood and about children duped by traffickers. She thinks she is the only one who knows about people without papers. Cocooned on the sofa, she now forgets to cook on her nights, a pastime she once loved. Lately, after the fiasco of wife number five, she seems to have convinced herself that her whole existence is nothing but a shadowy creation of some cruel fantasy.

The other day, I saw Arielle crying. I'd like to help her out, but she is difficult to talk to, and far too cerebral for me. She speaks quickly—as though speed equaled intelligence—while wobbling her glasses up and down disconcertingly. Anyway, what can I tell her? That these things are cyclical? When she moved in, my own mother was suffering, and before that it was Fatou, and before that it was Sylvie's turn. My father has always lived in a household filled with women. He can't let go of fantasies of womanhood and their romantic natures, despite soiled bathtubs filled with hair and lingerie floating in dirty water, and so he resorts to falling in love all over again. I know that Arielle feels cheated again this spring. Her eyes have opened, and she has lost faith. It has dawned on Arielle that my father might never see what she does, and she cannot afford to care.

Wife number five, there is nothing to say about her. She came, she left. She was young and pretty and insane. And one night, without warning, she tried to poison my father with a concoction of powdered herbs.

• • •

SOMETIMES I WONDER what we have done in this place but fill it with our prayers and our fighting. Here you will always find bottles of zem zem, and the amulet against the cross. At Easter time, we have come to celebrate Passover, too, because my best friend Charlotte is a Sephardic Jew from Morocco. In the fall, it's Ramadan, because my father is an old-fashioned guy from the back countries of the Moslem world. Madame Sylvie is a Catholic, but there are always the rituals, and the jumping over the coal, the incense cleansing, and other traditions from back home to keep us on the right path, and to keep my father from straying, again. I'll be leaving home soon, anyway.

I attend the local lycée. Louis-le-Grand is a sprawling, pristine white building filled from morning to early evening with sad kids whose fresh ideals become more and more jaded as they age. There is nothing much to describe there. The lycée is always the same. Sometimes there is an incendiary breeze of politics blowing through the school, but it doesn't last—it follows fashion. Students must still battle for their identities, to be a Jew, an Arab, or a Black, to prevent the slow death of brain cells from too much marijuana, wine, conversation, cigarettes, and cool.

Outside the lycée, we are nineteen-year-olds who should have left, but are held back one more year, because, well—because. We often meet each other by the Rond-Point, a red brick circular roundabout. The thin young girls smoke. They smoke, looking cool, preening for the older boys—who really have left school—as they tinker with their mopeds. They look energetic, lively, like they could be good for an afternoon of conversation, but they are lazy and unemployed. I smoke, too—Marlboros, cloves, small brown cigarettes—heavily, but I do it away from the scrutiny of my peers. I do it from the safe distance of Café Florian, a few blocks down from the lycée. Often, my best friend, Charlotte, joins me at the café, but I really prefer to luxuriate in my solitude. I tend to sit in the same spot until I remember that happiness need not be a memory, until I have a hot coffee and am thawed by ideas that take shape in solitude.

• • •

THE CAFÉ FLORIAN is owned by a couple who together have turned the café into my home away from home. Saul, a thin preppy New Yorker who was once a graphic designer, gave me my first designing gig when I was fifteen, by letting me do a flyer. I've designed their business cards, the menu, and the flyers. Designing things is what I love, and I'll offer ideas on anything—from the menus for the local cafés to murals on city walls to fabric that you can wear. When I was small, the strangeness of patterns and the deep textures within grainy shadows on walls brought me joy. It could also make me recoil. My mother used to yell at me, clapping her hands over her head when I would scream at the uneven trails left on my cereal bowl, the residues of lotion on her back: What is wrong with you?! *Now, design is just the way I subsidize my non-allowance.*

Saul is nostalgic, an American reinvention. You might think we would tire of America, but we don't. Café Florian is popular because of the Americana and American authors' books lining the walls—anyone can borrow them, even if we can't read them. There are more photographs of every American that has taken shelter in this city than you could want to name—from Baker to Miller to Saul himself. Saul's partner, Ibrahim, just looks like any old Berber, except he is Mauritanian. A middle-aged man with a soft gaze, he is content to let Saul host from his favorite corner, in his chair just next to the L titles, Little Women *and* Long Day's Journey into Night. *Meanwhile, Ibrahim flirts with the younger male art students from the nearby college. We can all sit in Café Florian, uninterrupted, nursing a cup of coffee or a glass of wine all day, if we want to. Ibrahim paints, too, and makes five-hour long documentaries on all this abstract stuff. My favorite sketch in the city is Ibrahim's. It is of a woman who languidly stretches out on a bed, surrounded by floating blue disembodied men. Her hair, chimney-smoke colored and curly, inches up to the ceiling and sails out the window. Ibrahim spoiled it a little by placing a quotation by Rimbaud at the painting's edge, to remind us that this dusky woman might just lead us, if we let her, to some African secret.*

Today, as always, when I come into Café Florian, Saul winks and smiles at me. "Salut, ça va?" And then, "Nice sneakers!"

Saul often prepares a café au lait *for me without asking, like a mother who knows that you need a glass of water, even when you don't know this yourself. Sometimes this is embarrassing, because I then deliberately say, "No, hot milk with brandy, instead," and he sighs, pushing the coffee toward me. "Have this on the house, too." Saul does things like this. He is gentle, and says to visitors,* Pay tomorrow. Pay when you can. Borrow a book. Peace. *It is because of Saul that I learned the words of so many American love songs.*

There are posters of African women above the register, with Rwandan coffee beans in baskets on their heads, juxtaposed with Vanity Fair *portraits and Russian posters. The kitchen is painted orange; the main café is red. While Saul is making today's coffee, I survey the Mexican plates of muffins behind the cold glass and tap my fingers to some gentle broken beats emerging from the speakers. There are mosaics above the* counter and a blackboard for things in French/English like granola, yogurt—food that is leaning toward vegetarianism. Nothing to eat, again.

"How is your father?" Saul asks, placing my coffee on the counter.

"Ahh . . . He has recovered. Yeah. Thanks for asking."

"What did he eat, man? How did that happen?"

"I'd rather not talk about it."

Saul's asking about my father has made me feel freshly upset, frustrated for some reason. I pick my coffee up from the counter and actually pretend that someone is calling on my cell phone. I rummage around my bag and feign surprise. I hate lying in these ways. I am convinced it's a moral malfunction.

"Okaaaay," he says slowly. Embarrassed, he changes the subject: "Did Ibrahim talk to you about the changes we need to make on the flyer before the reading?" I shake my head to myself. It's bad enough that I have to stay up at night writing all these English and French papers again.

"Saul. Can I do this after?" rotating my arm to mean some indefinite time in the future.

"We got to talk about the changes."

I shrug. "I'll do it, but my mother needs me this evening."

"Phewee." He dismisses my attitude. "Okaaaay, Antioch."

I walk past Claude, seated on the right side of the café. He is the resident unpublished writer. A mystery. I hear his murmured hello. Usually he stares over my head, fingers tapping on his keyboard, but I know that he secretly looks at all the women as they come into the café. I sense when we greet each other this afternoon that something different has passed between us. Could it be pity? He murmurs, "Nice sneakers." I pretend not to hear.

To his left, sitting by the window, is Monsieur Sissoko, the filmmaker, wearing his pajamas under flared jeans, his African leather slippers curled in Aladdin-like contentment under his table. As I pass his table, Monsieur Sissoko grabs at my shirt. His curly eyebrows converse with one another as if in the midst of a high-minded conversation of their own.

"Antioch, how is your father?"

I recall that Monsieur Sissoko almost kissed me last summer.

Nothing came of it. We were sitting outside of Café Florian; he was drinking heavily. He had just finished filming a documentary about prostitution in Addis Ababa, and he had been moved by it. He was telling me that, back in some mythical time, to love was to be honorable. I was listening to him. To love was to make someone smile. We got onto the subject of my family. And he began to insist that, though my father, Amadou Sy, was a good man, not all men make their hearts into marketplaces. I was listening to him, getting uncomfortable, for I knew that Sissoko and my mother were once friends. Did he mean for me to disrespect my father? No, no, he only meant that men who assert their love for more than one woman, who boast that they do so equally, do so at great cost. What kind of cost? I wanted to know. At one point, he murmured that I shouldn't be sad, and with a lump in my throat, I whispered that I wasn't. You must love your father, he muttered and lurched toward me in a kiss, but he must have seen how my eyes zoomed, because he pulled back, muttering, Sorry, sorry, sorry. Seeing him now is confusing.

"He is okay, much, much better in fact. Thank God."

"It must have been a shock. This kind of thing, going into the hospital at his age so suddenly, not knowing why, is so shocking."

"It is shocking, but not that shocking, you know?" I reply, an eyebrow mirroring his. "He ate something that nearly killed him. Life gives us knocks like this, reminds us that we are not permanent."

Monsiur Sissoko regards me pensively.

"But what? What? What could he have eaten?!" he throws his hands in the air indignantly. He shrugs his shoulder and puffs out his cheeks. "What could he have eaten here in Paris that would cause such a reaction?"

I consider his emotional reaction. "Horse meat or something. It was some disgusting meat that he ate."

My answer quiets him. "Monsieur Sissoko. You know what I find shocking?" I proceed to lie:

> That the whole thing was just made a lot worse by the fact that Baba has to deal with cancer, with a wife who just left him, and then he got food poisoning. He was rolling around with a stomachache when he collapsed in the bathtub, and, once he had fallen, he could not get himself up because he is getting far too old, so he pulled down the shower curtain and got burnt by the hot water. They make the tubs entirely too high, too high and too small in this country, that is what Madame Sylvie says, I guess, based on her experience of tubs in this country. When you are old or sick, uncle, it is hard to get in and out.

Puzzled, he leans forward, speaking in hushed staccato tones:

> And the new wife? Not one person has heard from her? Imagine that . . . Just married, and she leaves him, after everything he did to get her here, the gossip the man endured, and upsetting everyone else like that.

I think back to not so long ago, before wife number five became a reality. We did endure Arielle's madness, and Madame Sylvie's tight-lipped, African cloak-and-dagger silences. We endured many days of my father singing bawdy village songs while in the shower, knowing long before he told us that he did so with characteristic enthusiasm, contemplating the fresh flesh of a fifth wife.

"Does anyone know where she is? Has she gone home?"

"She is gone. Her mother was sick." Yallah, she never mattered.

I am amazed that those outside the family have already begun to connect her disappearance with my father's hospitalization. It happened two weeks ago. Already *people know, and because of the way our community is, there will be rumors and hints of foul play. Unavoidable. Sylvie, Fatou, and Arielle would enjoy telling this story to their friends. What can you expect when your existence is part of a collective, where each person of this freak show family has a confidante, who, in turn, will have two other friends listening to all the gory details? People should keep what they know to themselves.*

I came to Café Florian today to design a cover for a friend, not to get bogged down in the business of family. We are this community's only publicly polygamous family, although many of these men have their French wives here and their African wives back at home. Still, any mention of my father's many wives can make me hot with shame in the right instance. I make my way back to my table, wearing the famous Antioch grimace. I will now mentally and physically dissociate.

I regularly give leading roles to these men in my fantasies. In one of my fantasies, Claude and Monsieur Sissoko—without laptop and stripped of pajamas—pounce naked upon my young body, tear at me as I wind my way through the tables. Right there, in full view of everyone, they force me not to leave, and then they take me violently. (Monsieur Couché, was that less pornographic than my last composition?)

Usually, going to Café Florian is good for me. When I am not reading, devouring Balzac or someone else, then I am thinking of designing CD covers. Ordinarily I can't imagine the Antioch-who-lies-in-bed-all-day-depressed here. I take out my sketchbook and stare at the page for some time before long, winding green rivers in Vietnam snake their way into my mind. Is peace possible? Even though I feel tears welling up, is it not possible to dream here, to think here, to be cool here? Cool head, hot heart, even though my hands remain idle. This afternoon I feel restless. My thoughts are like ants in my head, my dreams like butterflies. I'm going back home.

• • •

From my bed, back in our apartment at 23 Boulevard du Temple, I ponder my future. Another teacher—not you, Monsieur Couché—a man I dream about, recently answered my prayers and called me at home. But, unfortunately for me, it was only to say that if I don't try harder this semester, I might have to re-do all my English literature papers next year. Hearing this made me cry at first. I rolled up into a ball on the floor and thought about how unfair that assessment was, because my trouble is not with English literature but with French. Palpitations. I remember being small and crowded against a wall by little red-faced, lispy-tongued children. Singe! Singe! French will always be the language of colonialism, while, for me at least, English remains the language of freedom. Strange that I'll probably fail both. All I have to show that I haven't been asleep is a few sketches and these notebooks.

• • •

ULTIMATELY, THE NEWS *is worthless anyway. There is no sense in being sad about it. My father has been sent to New York, and, when he gets better, we shall be moving there to start again. Again. Again . . . Such a strange word,* again. *It should summon repetition, but inside me, it summons change. You see, we move all the time. I change continents with the seasons. We're a diplomat's kids, but we never seem to live like the others do. For one thing, my father is a funny man. In fact, he is known for his humor, but he hardly ever smiles, not at home anyway. We are always much poorer than the others, living in rented accommodations in the shabbiest parts of town, eating nutrient-deficient meals. My mothers know nothing of the health revolution that has swept the Western world. We will be leaving 23 Boulevard du Temple for some hidden nook of Manhattan, except, unbeknownst to them, I'll be making my way directly to my own mother, who lives with a bunch of immigrants in Queens. For nine years I haven't lived with her. I respect that she chose her own life, settled in a land that welcomed her once as an exchange student.*

I have already begun to think about what freedom means. In the stillness of Café Florian, for instance, I've begun to think again about New York. Americans are free, after all, to express themselves in ways that we are not.

Love is or love isn't, *my brother Momo likes to say.*

I think about how I've never truly been in love.

I want to go to art school, but my father will never pay for that. "Art is for white men, homosexuals, at that," he says. In New York, you can pay your own way, I've been told.

I need to leave this family. Two weekends ago, Charlotte and I were invited to a party. Monsieur Sissoko had set up a huge projector screen in his loft in Montparnasse. All these artists were cooing and flexing, blocking our view of Sembène's Black Girl. *We shouldn't have even been there. I make flyers, and Charlotte is pretty. We didn't look too interesting, so nobody talked to us. We sat in a corner and watched the TV.*

Charlotte asked me, "Have you ever seen this film?"

"Too many times," I groaned. In fact, I had never seen that film before. It's true—I was glued to the screen and glad nobody came over. It reminded me of my mother's experience. Except she didn't come to my father's house from a village in Africa. She came from her Malian's mother's house right here in Paris. If you substitute that cruel white family for one of Africans you get her experience in my father's house: a life of drudgery and inequality.

On Saturdays, though, my mother welcomed the women who responded to her little paper advertisements for hair braiding. On those days, when Paris seemed full of promise, she put on her grandmother's Songhay music of Tinde drums, so that no one else in the house would understand. For her visitors, my mother tidied and cleaned those small, messy rooms we were always relegated to, first, in that apartment near Paris Opera; then near Château Rouge; and then on Boulevard de Rochechouart. My mother would come alive as she talked politics with leisurely women, women from the university, from offices, women from Africa and America and the Antilles, who had found her little ads in shops or on notice boards or through word of mouth, and who came to get their hair braided. I was too small to remember any one woman, but I do remember twirling long wisps of black and brown fake hair around my fingers like spider webs. I listened to these women break it down for her: that it was not normal to fight with people all the time. They listened, and they sympathized with her, and from them, I guess, she found some strength to follow her dream. By working part-time as a hair braider, my mother saved enough money to go to America to start a new life. Better that than her life back home, winnowing grain from her grand-mother's colorful baskets in front of a TV with a cigarette hanging out of her mouth. The only mark I can strike against her name is that she left me like a motherless calf in a crowd of angry elephant cows. My siblings might say differently, but this is what polygamy means to me: cruel abandonment.

A very long time ago, when I was a little girl, my father seemed to have a heart.

It was different for me, too, before. At least before I had my mother. Mine. She was different from the others, very different. She left our home triumphantly, even while in disgrace. My mother, my father's third wife after blind Fatou, thirty years his junior, was losing her mind. Married to someone with two wives already. What was she thinking? A black French girl in need of some identity, a woman who demurely listened to men she imagined were wiser than her. She became a drunkard while married to my father and his two wives. That is what they used to say. Often, I found her in a fetal position on the floor, I would lift her limp arm up to cover me. She no longer tried to be attractive to my elderly father, with sixty-one to her thirty years, and soon he forgot any obligation to her—and to me—and then he married Arielle. Even now, when he hears about my mother, he snorts, You are too young to know, but that woman, your mother, disgraced us. I don't understand. I can say a few bad things about my mother. The only disgrace, though, was the fighting she had to endure, the inner laceration of her heart, the lack of love. My father has a different story; Madame Sylvie has hers; and the neighborhood, I am sure, has its own.

• • •

I HAVE A MEMORY. I press my warm nose against the freezing glass. It is drizzling outside. But there she is, wobbling down the road, back on Friday at 2:00 AM, just as she promised. I look at how she totters, unsure of herself, so cold, her stupid, vain heels splitting the cobblestones at an hour when everyone else everywhere is warm and asleep. The Frenchman grabs at her face, he holds her tenderly in his arms as she throws back her head to laugh. He waits for her, stares at her as she totters drunkenly from his moped. I wonder if he will run after her a final time. He is a black leather-clad picture of chivalry. "Maman does not love him." I tap the words on the window, half hoping that she will hear and come to her senses.

Maman *does not love anyone, not even herself, I thump. She shivers. She is dressed only in her white fur jacket with the fist emblazoned on the back, in her tight blue jeans, her hair tucked in a huge patterned green headscarf. Her lips seem blue, her usually dark brown cheeks, pale. She sways, big-breasted. She takes faltering steps and is heavy on high heels.*

I squint at her and scratch my legs. She always teaches me that "only God is faithful to you." Because I am too little to understand this love, I think only of all the people who make me wary. I shuffle names in my mind like a jackpot machine. Maman *stops to smoke, shivering under a lamp before disappearing under the archway that leads to our apartment. I run into the corridor, stealthily, tiptoeing through molasses, so as not to alert anyone. They are already there, shelling peas at 1:45 AM around the kitchen table. Even worse, my father is pacing, a metal-like expression hardening on his face. Fresh accusations have simmered in her absence. If, for instance, my mother left the pot with sticky burned rice congealed at the bottom, Madame Sylvie would command, "Let it stay there. Zahara burned it. Let her wash it." Then, when Fatou does her share, palpating the hard nodules by mistake, her fingers recoil, and she curses Zahara through gritted teeth, not because she resents my mother, but because she cannot bear conflict. For days, this little pot, its crust hardening, sits by the sink. When the key has scraped at the hole a number of times, Fatou opens the door. She lets my mother know, in whispers, that she forgot to turn off the cooker again, that the oven blew open, that my father answered a call from a man, and that before she left, over seven days ago, in one of her tempers, she forgot to apologize to Madame Sylvie for slamming all the doors. She says it all in hushed tones, just to let her know what to expect, because she cares for my mother much more than the others do.*

• • •

*"*Antioch, the car *is ready."*

I cringe when I hear the voice of Madame Sylvie. Her voice makes my skin pimple. In the room that I share with my little sisters, I burrow down into my rumpled bed. When she calls a second time, I raise myself on my elbows but remain under my sheets, staring into darkness. The floorboards bend under her feet. She annoys me more and more with each approaching word.

"Antioch, answer! Why does this girl never answer when she is called?"

Well, I hate the way she says my name, the way it hangs in the back of her throat like phlegm. She pronounces it coldly, conjuring an artless city, and it's a town, my mother's favorite town in the whole world, a gentle and friendly place. A college town in Ohio, where she spent a year. I wait some more.

*"*Maman, *you may enter. I am in my room," I say in my most quiet voice, and then I throw a coughing fit. Madame Sylvie opens the door. On her pinhead she wears a fake-lace wrapper, and she has pencil where her eyebrows should be.*

I can say a few kind things about Madame Sylvie. I will say them, for otherwise you might be misled. One good thing is that she knows what Mohammed is really like. He's my favorite brother, the sole vessel of my father's affection right now, but a cad just the same.

Another good thing is that, were it not for some dreg of maternal feeling, leading to her concrete intervention, I would have been sent at age nine by my father to live in Senegal with relatives, once that useless woman who is my own mother had left. Moreover, somewhere in this pit of resentment is the faint possibility that we don't have to be enemies, that we could perhaps even be friends. Once Madame Sylvie confiscated one of my Egyptian feminist books. I caught her later, sitting at my father's desk, engrossed with the story of Doria Shafik, a young philosophy graduate of the Sorbonne who fought for Egyptian women's civil liberties. Madame Sylvie often borrows my books.

Before she bore the accolade of senior wife, Madame Sylvie was, in her own right, a distinguished woman, a chemist. Sylvie Tidjane was something to behold, I think. In a black-and-white picture of her graduation, she is a Junoesque woman standing over six feet tall. Her huge wrapper shades the female chemists lined up behind her; her face is rounder than it is now, and her shy, youthful smile is a promise of the future, a reminder that, once upon a time, African girls ran from the village to the modern world, too. She was among the first Senegalese women who went to university abroad. She had a brain, but then she married my father. I find it hard to understand, but I guess my father was a different man then. Back then, he cavorted with poets. He laughed, Madame Sylvie says, made a joke out of everything, made her forgive every looming sign. When they first met in Paris, he relied on her, promised to build a life with her, sent money to her sister, even promised fidelity. He believed that Africa was a She, a blessed woman. He believed, like others of his generation, that he would break with the past. He was a dutiful son and had something to say.

I sometimes think that my father was deluded. He may have fought against Africa under colonialism, and today he might fight for Africa's future, but somehow he never fought to understand himself. Africa will always remains a timid She, lying supine at his boot. As my father likes to say,

> The challenge for women in Africa is to balance the demands and
> needs of the modern world with the importance of our customary
> laws. They reproduce the culture; they teach the norms. If not for
> the women, then where would our culture and traditions be?

What does he mean? With age, my father fills out the stereotypes easily. But, thankfully, I am not his wife; I am his daughter, and my father still can make me smile.

Madame Sylvie has become a bitter woman. Marriage has cast a pallor, especially when my father took not only one more wife, but three on her watch, according to his rights under Islamic law, and also our tradition. Now, Madame Sylvie further dulls the senses she has left by wearing cheap perfume. She spends her time trying to run a household, trying to control her husband's legendary levels of lust, trying to raise children who are not hers. She has to look attractive, but she has become very fat from all of the worrying and very spotty from all of the bleach. She is patient, but cynicism pervades her actions, and she resents us. It is a fact, and we all know it. My father can be spectacularly cruel—but why tell it all now? Patience is torturous but necessary. Madame Sylvie has never been rewarded for her suffering, and she never will be. Look how the shape of her soul has become altered. Nobody steals panties, or reads through private papers and knows the timing of menstruation and pregnancies like her. She exists to control us. She tells her own wasted time by our furtive movements.

"You had better be ready."

Today my father was supposed to give his annual speech at the embassy. But a Mauritanian academic has been hastily called out as a substitute. Madame Sylvie will preface whatever he has to say with an apology, an explanation, and a summary of my father's work. We must still attend, or else suffer the inevitable gossip. More substandard rhetoric from another suit who can outtalk the French, who must represent. Who really cares? We must.

The floorboards bend under her feet. She grunts.

"Antioch, Antioch, Antioch! Yallah?!" she throws open the door, stares at me napping in the dark. She throws back my sheets, her pointy, angular face suspicious.

"Why don't you go without me, Maman? I'm not feeling very well," I quickly say, and resume my cough. I imagine the space to finish designing the CD cover for my friend DJ Shi Wan.

Although she usually speaks impeccable French, when she gets irritated, Madame Sylvie claps her hands and widens her wild eyes and reverts to Wolof, deep and guttural. Like all African languages, tone is very important, and right now her tone is very clear.

"Never mind your coughing. Get in the fucking car. Why has God saddled me with an extra girl?"

I will go this one time. Afterward, I'll tell my father what I think. I will tell him that one day I will decide for myself and will leave everything that comes with him— his children, his wives, his in-laws—behind. I drag myself out of the room to the bathroom, throw back my million-and-one dyed-red braids into a bun, and put kohl on my eyes. I like my eyes—they are stubborn, like my mother's. My father told me that. I sigh and look at all the female products lying around the bathroom. It is falling to bits; the ceiling is peeling, and the black patches of fungus are spreading. In the center of the bathtub is a bowl of soaking underwear. I think it is disgusting, until I notice the patterns on one of them. They are mine. Mine as in belong to me, difficult to imagine in a polygamous household: everything belongs to everyone. Are we meant to share everything? Madame Sylvie has ordered the cleaning lady to wash my underwear, without my permission. I am nineteen years old.

When I confide in Charlotte, she usually says, "Imagine what your mother would say in this situation." *She knows about this, because her mother died when she was a little girl, so she does this sort of imagining all the time.*

"In *this situation! I don't know. I just can't imagine her saying anything.*"

"*Come on. It's good to hear her voice in your head speaking and listening to just you, giving only you her blessings.*"

She is right. Mothers know these things. My mother, though, is missing in action in a world of unknowns. Yet, sometimes I do hear her voice: What are you going to do Antioch, now that your sandcastle is starting to dissolve under a rolling wave? Don't build it so close to the tide, again!

I whisper to myself, Poor you! At least I'm going to get out of here.

"*What did you just say?*"

"*Nothing,* Maman, *just need to do my teeth.*"

• • •

Semi-autobiographical you say? No, Monsieur Couché. This is one hundred percent *Antioch Sy.* ◉

African Studies and Universities since Independence

the challenges of epistemic and institutional decolonization

Paul Tiyambe Zeleza

IN MARCH 1957, two important events took place in the political and intellectual histories of Africa. One happened on the continent itself: the declaration of independence of Ghana; the other, in the United States: the formation of the African Studies Association (ASA). Both were products of the momentous struggles for decolonization and symbolic of Africa's changing presence in the worlds of international affairs and knowledge production. The decolonization of Ghana opened the floodgates of African independence; the formation of the ASA fortified Africanist scholarship in the world's most powerful nation.

Despite their obvious connections, the two events represented divergent historical trajectories culminating in the consecration of *black* political autonomy and *white* intellectual authority. Ghana was not the first African country to gain independence from colonial rule in the twentieth century—that honor belongs to Libya, which achieved independence in December 1951, or perhaps Egypt, which became self-governing in 1922. Similarly, the thirty-six (predominantly white) Africanists who founded the ASA in New York were not the first scholars to study Africa seriously; African American scholar-activists hold that distinction. The preeminence given to Ghana in the pantheon of African independence and the ASA in the annals of African studies betrays the braided racialized histories of African independence and African studies: the construction of Africa as *black*, a truncation of the continent to its sub-Saharan components, a paradigm that is sanctified in Eurocentric historiography and faithfully reproduced in Africanist scholarship.

Ghana's achievement of independence and the formation of the ASA marked a critical moment—still very far from completion—in Africa's age-old drive to decolonize its political and knowledge economies. In both cases, the fifty-odd years since have witnessed remarkable developments marked by impressive successes and ignoble failures. This has been the story of African universities on the continent and African studies around the world. Insofar as the bulk of African universities were established and African studies spread to most parts of the world following independence, the fates of universities within and African studies outside the continent continue to be interlocked, as they were in 1957.

This is, of course, not to claim that little has changed. Over the last fifty years, African studies and African universities have undergone many twists and turns as both have expanded from their rather modest beginnings. Today, both are vast enterprises encompassing thousands of colleges and supporting institutions—from publishers to conferences to consultancies—that cater to millions of students, faculty, and staff in the Americas, Europe, and Asia. Predictably, the institutional, intellectual, and ideological dynamics and tendencies of African studies and African universities are exceedingly difficult to analyze, in part because of the very complexity of their interconnections, reinforced by the globalization of higher education.

Even a cursory glance reveals that the landscape of African higher education is more variegated than ever before. It consists of institutions that are public and private; secular and religious; comprehensive and specialized; large and small; transnational and parochial; research intensive and vocational; and whose composition of faculty, students, and staff varies in terms of gender, class, and other defining social markers, as do their relations with the state, economy, and society. Similarly, the global African studies field has grown and been transformed as its social composition—the racial, gender, generational, and national identities of its members—has changed. Scholarly agendas have expanded and become more complex, with shifting disciplinary and interdisciplinary configurations and the periodic emergence of new theoretical, thematic, and topical interests. The processes and structures of knowledge production have responded to the massive reorganization of universities, the publishing industry, and the technologies of information dissemination and consumption. The public and political charges and constituencies of academic communities have adjusted to complicated and contradictory transformations in African and global political economies and ideologies.

Developments within and outside Africa—in African universities and African studies programs overseas—influence each other in obvious and sometimes oblique ways. The flows of influence are multiple in their directions and levels. The institutionalization of African studies around the world in the 1950s and 1960s cannot be divorced from the processes of African nationalism and decolonization, which raised the political and paradigmatic profile of the new independent states for foreign policy makers and higher education institutions.

Several decades later, the crisis of African universities in the 1980s and 1990s led to the migration of thousands of African academics to universities in the global North, which changed the social composition and intellectual terrain of the field. Along the way, Africanists in the Anglophone world exported and imported theoretical and methodological frameworks from other parts of the world. Africanists were inspired by the works of Latin American dependency theorists, French postmodernist thinkers, Indian subaltern historians, and African feminists, to mention only a few examples. The processes of contemporary globalization—intensified flows of capital, commodities, and cultures across communities, countries, and continents—have reinforced the universalizing ambitions and propensities of universities. Globalization is simultaneously producing new contexts and imperatives for intellectual communities, thus increasing transnational intellectual flows and engagements.

• • •

ONE CAN EXAMINE the developments of African studies and African universities since independence in terms of both *moments* and *models*. Defining *moments* entails identifying dominant tendencies. Periodization is fundamental to the craft of historians, essential to historical explanation and coherence; it contextualizes events and processes, giving them meaning and importance, and conditions our images of the past; it generates many of the theories and abstractions that sustain historical discourse, thus defining the protocols of scholarly production and turf among historians. Periodization is the essence of historicity, albeit always difficult to construct, because of the complex interplay of intellectual, institutional, and ideological dynamics. Three broad periods can be discerned in the development of African universities: the *golden era*, the *crisis era*, and the *recovery era*.

The golden era, which lasted from the 1950s to the late 1970s, was characterized by the excitement of building new universities and expanding old ones, all underpinned by the triumph of African nationalism and the euphoria of independence. During this era, vigorous efforts were made to decolonize the disciplines, to strip them of their Eurocentric cognitive and civilizational conceits. But no sooner had African universities consolidated themselves than their institutional and intellectual standing began to erode as a result of pecuniary and political crises brought about by the rising tide of austerity—or neo-liberal economic restructuring—and authoritarianism, especially pronounced from the late 1970s to the late 1990s. Since then, recovery has begun in some countries, as the recessions of development and democracy have been halted and are even being reversed with renewed economic growth and political liberalization. The era of recovery is still in its early phases, for African universities continue to face severe challenges.

Identifying scholarly tendencies for African studies is equally challenging. Institutionally, African studies has been included within existing disciplines or else seen as an independent discipline or "interdiscipline" in the humanities and social sciences, manifested in various organizational forms: departments, centers, institutes, or programs. Ideologically, it has exhibited imperial, solidarity-promoting, and liberatory tendencies. Intellectually, African studies has been dominated by culturalist, developmentalist,

Kwaku,
Assimilation
in Transition.
2008. Mixed
media, 57 ×
74 inches

deconstructionist, and globalist imperatives. Needless to say, these moments and trends manifest themselves quite differently in different countries and world regions, as the political economies of knowledge production are often highly spatialized. Knowledge systems and paradigms are mediated and mapped by the unyielding demands of historical geography. For this reason, the three moments identified for African universities cannot be expected to be replicated in other world regions. Yet there have been broad global trends. A global framework is useful not only because we live in an increasingly globalized world, but also because it enables us to transcend the myopic tendency to envelop developing and developed countries—in Africa and the rest of the world—in mystificatory exceptionalisms.

In many parts of the world, including Europe and the Americas, the mid-1970s marked the end of the long postwar boom, which was followed by the neoliberal era of slow growth, and the dismantling of the welfare state in the global North and the developmentalist state in the global South. The consequences for social sectors such as higher education were predictably severe: cutbacks in fiscal support for public education led to the expansion of private universities and the privatization of public universities. Since the 1980s, there has been a widespread perception that public universities as institutions, and academia as a profession, are facing unprecedented crises brought about by globalization. Rapid technological, economic, political, and sociocultural transformations emanating from both the wider world and academia itself are eroding the old systems, structures, and stabilities of higher education. Powerful internal and external forces—as much peda-gogical and paradigmatic as they are pecuniary, political, and demo-graphic—are reconfiguring all aspects of university life constituted around the triple mission of teaching, research, and service. Battles of various kinds and intensities are being waged within and outside university systems over missions and mandates, legitimacy and status as producers, disseminators, and consumers of scientific and scholarly knowledge.

• • •

THE POSTCOLONIAL UNIVERSITY was founded to promote the dreams of African nationalism: decolonization and development. Both the political class and the intelligentsia saw these as essential for achieving and sustain-ing African self-determination. Thus, in the heady years immediately fol-lowing independence, academics were as intoxicated as the politicians by the tantalizing and totalizing dreams of building their new nations, of refashioning their place in a world that had long exploited and oppressed them. New universities were founded; old regional universities were dis-mantled and reconstituted as national universities; and growing numbers of academics—many of them returning from overseas with hard-earned degrees, eager to reshape their societies—happily joined the ranks of the expanding middle classes. This was the golden era, before relations between the new rulers and restive intellectuals turned sour, and African universities fell on hard times.

During the colonial period, the imperial tendency had predominated in both Africa and the few overseas institutions that deemed it even worthwhile to teach about Africa. Whatever its other objectives, colonialism was not an educational enterprise, as evidenced by the fact that it left behind very few universities in Africa—indeed, the majority of countries did not have even a single university at inde-pendence. The few colonial universities were established rather belatedly, during the twi-light years of empire, as a means of producing skilled professionals to serve a maturing colonial capitalism and save it from the dangerous agitation of the nationalist masses. Small and elitist, colonial universities were unapologeti-cally Eurocentric, patterned on the metropolitan universities from which they drew much of their faculty and curricula. African history was not even taught, for African societies were supposed to have had no history before the "civiliz-ing mission" of the European conquest. At best, Africa was the subject of anthropological folklore.

South Africa was one of the few countries with a sizeable university system, although higher education was racially segregated almost from the

> **Academics were as intoxicated as the politicians by the tantalizing and totalizing dreams of building their new nations.**

Kwaku, *Stand On Your Own.* 2006. Mixed media, 38 x 38 inches

beginning. The introduction of apartheid in 1948 reinforced the iron grid of racial inequality in education, as blacks were no longer allowed to attend the "white" universities without special government approval, and separate universities were created for Africans in the so-called self-governing home-lands and for "Coloreds" and Indians in the major cities. If the white universities were unapologetically Eurocentric, the black universities were irredeemably condemned to the mediocrity of Bantu education. And when African studies was introduced in the white universities—as Mahmood Mamdani observed in his trenchant critique of African studies at Univeresity of Cape Town in 1998—it was really *Bantu* studies, focusing on Bantu administration, customary law, Bantu languages and anthropology. The "Africa" of Bantu studies, like that of Euroamerican African studies, was confined to the Hegelian construct of tropical, equatorial, black, sub-Saharan Africa.

Only in independent Africa did the liberatory thrust of African studies—first developed in the diaspora—find an auspicious home, as the newly independent states sought to undo a century of colonial educational neglect and to decolonize African studies. The expansion of higher education after independence was phenomenal: hundreds of universities were established, and the number of university students skyrocketed from 120,000 in 1960 to 3.5 million by 1995. The postcolonial universities were much larger in size than their colonial predecessors, broader in their missions, and they expanded their disciplinary and curricula offerings. The new universities were designed as engines of socioeconomic transformation and centers of epistemic emancipation, as the African intelligentsia readily rediscovered and rewrote their peoples' histories and humanity so cruelly seized and denied by Europe.

The emancipatory mission of African studies was unambiguously articulated by Ghana's first President, Kwame Nkrumah, when he opened the Institute of African Studies at the University of Ghana in 1961, and when he addressed the first Congress of Africanists in Accra in 1962. Nkrumah, a Pan-Africanist, urged his academic audience to produce genuine knowledge about Africa through scientific and academic rigor—knowledge that would promote Africa's development and transformation—and to share their discoveries with the rest of the world. Nkrumah was schooled in the civil rights struggles of the segregated diaspora and the nationalist struggles of colonial Africa, and he was passionately committed to Africa's regeneration in all spheres.

Over the next four decades, the struggles for intellectual decolonization scored uneven victories across Africa. The multiple developmental crises engendered by structural adjustment programs in the 1980s and 1990s also affected higher education, gravely undermining the liberatory capacities and commitments of African universities and intellectuals. The divorce between academia and the state commenced when the technocratic agenda assigned to the universities—to produce skilled professionals and workers for the indigenization of the state bureaucracy and the "formal" economy—was increasingly achieved, a success due in part to the small size of most African countries and economies and the deceleration of economic

Only in independent Africa did the liberatory thrust of African studies—first developed in the diaspora—find an auspicious home.

growth from the mid-1970s on. To the overseers of the state, whose incapacity to deliver the fruits of *uhuru* [independence] became increasingly evident, the university had not only lost its mission, but was becoming a potentially dangerous site populated by volatile educated youths and devious academics who reveled in purveying "foreign ideology" and "irrelevant" theoretical research. During the lost decade of the 1980s, state-sanctioned anti-intellectualism found succor in the strange gospel from the World Bank, that Africa needed primary schools rather than universities. Meanwhile, the influx of expatriates lowered the short-term costs of neglecting African universities and the concomitant emigration of skilled labor, including academics. By the late 1990s, there were an estimated 100,000 expatriates working in Africa—at a cost of $4 billion—almost equal to the number of skilled Africans who had left.

In this context, the liberatory mission of the postcolonial university gave way to the imperatives of survival, as middle-class comforts slipped from the lives of academics in many countries. Diminishing resources, combined with mounting state tyranny, led to the deterioration of research, teaching, and physical infrastructures; the demoralization of faculty and students; and a social devaluation of the status of academics and the scholarly enterprise. The "brain drain"—or "brain hemorrhage"—from the universities to other sectors at home, or to universities abroad, intensified. Many academics became consultancy hustlers and informal sector hawkers and hacks. But another, more productive response to the crisis was the establishment by prematurely retired or part-time university academics of an intellectually vibrant and autonomous academic NGO sector comprising continental, subregional, and national research networks and organizations.

• • •

THE AFRICAN UNIVERSITY crisis shifted the primacy of knowledge production in African studies—which had belonged to African institutions for a brief, exciting period during the golden era—to universities in the global North, especially the United States, where by the 1970s the field was firmly anchored in area studies. Before the development of the area studies model in the late nineteenth and early twentieth centuries, African studies was largely confined to the historically black colleges and universities (HBCUs) and dominated by African American scholar-activists. The post–World War II, Cold War era marked the second phase in the development of the field, when the gravity of African studies shifted toward European American scholars and historically white universities bankrolled by foundations and the federal government's Title VI programs. The end of the Cold War ushered in the third phase, when a vigorous assault was launched against area studies, including African studies, and their viability on U.S. campuses appeared threatened.

Four major critiques were advanced against area studies, each of which was vigorously and sometimes effectively rebutted by area studies practitioners. First, it was argued that the idea of area studies was a Cold War political project that had now outlived its usefulness. Second, area studies were said by scholars such as David Szanton (in *The Politics of Knowledge: Area Studies and the Disciplines* [2004]) to be "merely 'ideographic,' primarily concerned with description, as opposed to the 'nomothetic' or theory building and generalizing character of the core social science disciplines."

Others maintained that area studies scholars uncritically propagated the universalizing or localizing categories, perspectives, commitments, and theories of their imperialist interlocutors in the metropoles and their nativist informants in the postcolonies. Champions of globalization contended that the "new world order" of enhanced transnational economic, cultural, information, and demographic flows rendered the old structures for organizing and producing knowledge in bounded regions increasingly obsolete. What was now required, in the place of old-fashioned area studies, it was argued, were international or global studies or, at the very least, comparative regional studies.

The Social Science Research Council (SSRC) abolished its area studies committees in 1996 and foundations duly withdrew their funding support for area studies and launched new initiatives on cross-regional and globalization issues. But the American triumphalism of the 1990s was brought to a sudden halt by the terrorist attacks of September 11, 2001, which made it clear that history was not over after all, and foreign cultures still existed that demanded understanding—translation—on their own terms. Thus began the fourth phase, marked by renewed expansion of area studies programs, as universities embraced the national security imperative of the state and rediscovered the importance of educational internationalization. Universities that had never hired Africanists before suddenly began to do so. Ironically, some of the larger and older African studies centers—such as those at Columbia, UCLA, Boston University, and Northwestern—began to face challenges of leadership and direction and saw their programs shrink.

Historically, in the United States, both imperial and liberatory tendencies have coexisted and competed most fiercely. The presence of a large African diaspora is the primary reason for this. The United States is currently home to nearly 40 million people of African descent, who, if they were a country, would be Africa's sixth most populous (after South Africa). On the one hand, knowledges of Africa are a part of the arsenal of imperial hegemony for the world's lone—and until recently rather lonely—superpower. Indeed, conventional histories of African studies, such as the one commissioned by the ASA and produced by Jane Guyer in 1996, attribute the development of African studies to the historically white universities, where it is said the field emerged after World War II to serve the national security agenda of the United States, then embroiled in superpower rivalry with the Soviet Union to win hearts and minds in the Third World.

September 11, 2001, made it clear that history was not over after all, and foreign cultures still existed that demanded understanding—translation—on their own terms.

While this narrative is correct as far as the historically white universities that currently dominate African studies are concerned, it ignores the origins of the field in the HBCUs before the white universities discovered African studies in the context of the Cold War. African studies as an academic field was pioneered by Howard, not Northwestern, and by W. E. B. Du Bois, rather than Melville Herskovits. The Africa of African American activist-scholars focused on Africa's global civilizational status, the

Kwaku,
Akoma Asem
1 (A Heart's
Matter). 2008.
Mixed media,
23 x 25 inches

Continent as a whole, and its diasporic connections. In contrast, the Africa of professional Africanists became increasingly prescriptive, focusing on Africa's deficiencies and that strange contraption called "sub-Saharan Africa."

Ironically, the civil rights movement, which brought more African studies and African American studies programs to U.S. campuses, led to an institutional and racial split in African studies, as African American scholars gravitated and were pushed to African American studies, and African studies came to be dominated by European American scholars. More recently, yet another Africa has emerged in the American academy, that of continental African scholars who relocated in growing numbers, from the 1980s on, as African universities faced the crisis of structural maladjustment, thanks to the misdirected policies of the international financial institutions unwisely followed by African leaders. These scholars brought with them the preoccupations and anxieties of postcolonial Africa.

Thus, there are now at least three "Africas" in the American academy, each with its own history, and this has made contestations within African studies complex and fierce. The imperial and liberatory tendencies have jostled for supremacy for the last half century. In the twenty-first century, following the terrorist attacks of September 11, we are back to the security imperative that guided area studies at the height of the Cold War, and the imperial tendency frames funding formulas of area studies, including African studies, by state agencies and private foundations. At the same time, however, the Africana studies movement and the diaspora studies movement are reconfiguring the study of Africa, forcing new realignments within the American academy among Africanists and Africans, including engagements between them and the institutions and intellectual communities based on the continent.

· · ·

AMONG THE COLONIAL powers of Western Europe, the imperial tendency has predominated with little domestic contestation. Knowledge of Africa, however distorted or self-serving, was of course an essential part of the colonial project, although courses in African studies were systematically introduced into British, French, Belgium, and Portuguese universities after World War II. In fact, the first lectureship in Africa history was set up at the University of London's School of Oriental and African Studies (a name it adopted in 1938 after having been called the "School of Oriental Studies" from its formation in 1916). Empire and its aftermath continue to structure African studies in these countries, notwithstanding the differences of national intellectual traditions. African studies developed and became a *bona fide* discipline within the former colonial powers

African studies developed and became a *bona fide* discipline within the former colonial powers because of the existence of the Africa of colonial memory.

because of the existence of the Africa of colonial memory. Such countries have found it particularly difficult to incorporate the other Africas within and the African diasporas—largely created out of empire—ensconced within the former colonial powers' borders. African studies remains there, by and large, the study of the colonial and postcolonial "other."

Not surprisingly, African intellectual voices—whether those of the historic diasporas or the recent immigrants of structural adjustment—remain muted in much of the West European academy. Francophone scholars have been trekking to the Anglophone world, especially the United States, rather than France, because of restrictive French immigration policies and institutional racism. The relocated Francophone scholars are forced to produce works in English, which are not readily translated in France. (For example, V. Y. Mudimbe's canonical text, *The Invention of Africa*, published in 1988, has yet to be translated into French.) Yet, Anglophone scholars happily imbibe, and enjoy becoming intoxicated with, translated French high theory. Intellectual inhospitality is, of course, not a failing peculiar to Gallic conceit. Good old Britain faces similar challenges of

Kwaku, *Akoma Asem 2.* 2008. Mixed media, 23 x 24 inches

how to develop more equitable and productive relations between not only white and black British Africanists but also the African academics who have migrated to Britain since the 1990s. Scholars of African descent often complain bitterly of their professional and textual exclusion from the African studies canon.

Germany offers a peculiar case, as a colonial power that lost its African empire after World War I. In Germany, African studies has exhibited a complex amalgam of imperial and solidarity tendencies, especially if we consider the two Germanys of the post–World War II era. Scholarship in West Germany continued the long colonial tradition of studying African languages and cultural areas, themes that echoed more general scholarly preoccupations with German migrations and cultural formation. In East

Germany, in contrast, Africanist scholarship expressed Marxist solidarities with Africa's oppressed classes and nations.

If the operations, legacies, and imperatives of imperialism structured African studies in Britain and France, and more ambivalently in Germany, the impulses of solidarity have been most evident in Sweden and Russia, as well as in parts of Asia. Swedish interest in Africa and African studies was motivated by the needs of small-power global diplomacy, specifically, political solidarity with the liberation movements in southern Africa and economic support for development cooperation, which was spawned by the ideological correspondence between the Swedish social welfare state project and the developmentalist state projects in the new African states. In the Soviet Union, African studies flourished, predicated on support for African anticolonial struggles and postindependence development and social transformation, and driven by the shifting preoccupations of Soviet Marxism and the nation's superpower status. Since the collapse of the Soviet Union, the solidarity imperative in African studies in Russia has waned, even if—or perhaps because—the field has become freer from ideological controls.

Brazil developed the myth of "racial democracy" following the failures of the "whitening" project of the late nineteenth and early twentieth centuries.

As for Asia, the solidarity imperative prevails in African studies in India and China. The development of African studies in India from the mid-1950s on owes much to the internationalist vision of India's leaders, especially Mohandas Gandhi and Jawaharlal Nehru, both of whom were Africanists in their own right. India's independence leaders believed fervently in Afro-Asian liberation and resurgence, and stressed the need for a clear and critical understanding of the world, hence the imperative to develop a cadre of academic specialists on various world regions. The establishment of African studies in China from the late 1950s on resulted from expanding ties between Africa and China in the aftermath of African decolonization and the Chinese revolution, and shared visions against European imperialism and for rapid development. As in India, there was strong ideological and fiscal support from the state for African studies programs. In China, African studies grew from a politically oriented to an academically oriented inter-discipline and gradually expanded the range of its thematic and topical focus and disciplinary coverage.

In none of these countries did African studies develop out of liberatory impulses, that is, in order to produce Africanist knowledge for the empowerment and emancipation of marginalized and racialized national citizens, an impulse most pronounced in the Americas, among African diasporas, and within Africa itself. Race and racial hierarchies have been foundational for the settler societies of the Americas. They frame the political and cultural economies of social life and public and scholarly discourses. The role

Kwaku, *Stand Together.* 2006. Mixed media, 34 x 34 inches

of *domestic* liberation politics in the development of African studies is readily apparent in Brazil and the Caribbean, as well.

Brazil has the largest African diaspora population in the world—an estimated 85 million. As President Luiz Inácio Lula da Silva likes to say when meeting with African leaders, Brazil is the second most populous African country, after Nigeria! From the 1930s on, Brazil developed the myth of "racial democracy" following the failures of the "whitening" project of the late nineteenth and early twentieth centuries. Afro-Brazilian activists and scholars began to mobilize the population to fight for a new dispensation that would promote racial equality. Specifically, demands were made for the teaching of African history and the history of Africans long ignored in Brazilian historiography, which disregarded the enormous contributions of Africans in the formation of the country. In 2003, a law was passed making compulsory the teaching of Afro-Brazilian and African history and culture. This was a struggle to produce and disseminate complex, critical, and empowering histories of Africa and Brazil, recognizing the historicity and humanity of Africans and Afro-Brazilians, and incorporating Afro-Brazilian connections to both Africa and the other Afro-American diasporas.

Many of the Caribbean islands have African diaspora majorities, but from slavery and colonialism they developed insidious ideologies of racial disparagement against Africa and Africanness or blackness. Consequently, African studies formally developed as a part of the wave of the black power movement and collective self-refashioning that followed independence, in the 1960s. The introduction of African studies in schools and institutions of higher learning emerged alongside an age-old popular, organic African presence and intellectual tradition embodied in the work of Caribbean intellectuals on African societies, cultures, and history. Most of these intellectuals were activists as well, ranging from Marcus Garvey and George Padmore to C. L. R. James, Frantz Fanon, and Arthur Lewis, who made significant contributions to Pan-Africanism and global intellectual movements.

• • •

WHAT ARE THE intellectual tendencies exhibited in African studies and African universities, the dominant paradigms through which African phenomena and processes have been filtered and analyzed? Again, at the risk of oversimplification, I have identified four typologies: the *culturalist, developmentalist, deconstructionist*, and *globalist*. The culturalist tradition is characteristic of perspectives in the humanities; the developmentalist and globalist traditions are more emblematic of approaches in the social sciences; the deconstructionist tradition straddles both.

African studies was originally the province almost exclusively of anthropology, the premier colonial science, which, through its structuralist-functionalist paradigms and ethnographic present, froze African societies in static "tribalized" enclaves. Banished from much of the postcolonial academy with the advent of decolonization, anthropology was accused of exonerating colonialism of the cultural, cartographic, and cognitive violence it wreaked on Africa. The discipline entered into a period of deep epistemic, ethical, and political crisis as it tried to rescue itself from its discredited colonial complicity. It has yet fully to recover.

Elsewhere in the global North, as the discipline slowly renewed itself, anthropology became more historical, more global, and more reflexive, so that even if the ethnographic method retained its foundational supremacy for the discipline, and the romance with the "local" persisted, African cultures were increasingly expanded in scale, time, and connectedness to each other and to international cultural flows. In the process, African cultures lost some of their apparent timelessness, essentialism, and exoticism, and Africans as groups and individuals could at last begin to escape from the suffocating confines of stable and static "traditional," "kinship," and "lineage" systems. Critics such as Archie Mafeje (*The Theory and Ethnography of African Social Formations*, 2002) have maintained that, while it is possible

It is doubtful whether anthropology can be deracialized in its study of the "other," and fully escape its racial, racializing, and racist past.

Kwaku,
Waitin' in
Vain. 2006.
Mixed media,
34 × 34 inches

to deconstruct colonial anthropology, it is doubtful whether anthropology can be deracialized in its study of the "other," and fully escape its racial, racializing, and racist past.

The culturalist tradition in African studies is, of course, not confined to anthropology as a discipline or to Eurocentric approaches. The vindication-ist tradition of African diaspora scholars from the eighteenth century—who tried to vigorously defend the historicity of Africa and the humanity of Africans against the scientific racism emerging out of the hideous entrails of plantation slavery—rested on culturalist premises: that African cultures and societies were normal, not primitive aberrations; that they were civiliza-tions, complex societies. The vindicationist tradition mutated into the nationalist tradition, most fully developed in nationalist historiography, which bloomed following decolonization and found its most auspicious home in Africa's new or old, decolonized universities. African history ceased to be taught as a story of lack and becoming—lacking and becoming Europe—and scholars painstakingly sought to unravel African activities, adaptations, choices, and initiatives. While nationalist historiography was more enamored of political than of cultural history as such, its civilizational argument against Europe—against colonialism—was fundamentally a cultural one. This Afrocentric analytical impulse exercised a powerful influence on African and Africanist scholarship, inspiring a whole range of disciplinary studies, from African languages and literatures to religions and philosophies. This impulse finds expression in contemporary South Africa in the indigenous knowledge systems movement.

The culturalist tradition found a worthy competitor in developmentalism, which emerged after World War II from a conjunction of several forces. There were the nationalists who prayed at the altar of development—for nationalism was, in part, a struggle for development, for the material advancement of African societies, for improved standards of living. The language of development was also used by the African political class to mobilize the impoverished and restive masses. For the beleaguered colonial powers, development served as a handy substitute for the tattered rhetoric of civilization discredited by the horrendous barbarism of World War II, and as a plea against nationalist charges of colonial exploitation. In the meantime, the discovery and problematization of poverty and backwardness in Africa, Asia, and Latin America—collectivized into the "Third World" in the 1950s—turned development into a global industry overseen by newly created international financial institutions, agencies, and civil society organizations.

Developmentalism became a powerful paradigm in African universities across the continent and in African studies programs abroad, as disciplines ranging from sociology to political science and economics, the "queen" of the social sciences, devised ever more sophisticated and prescriptive models to examine African societies, polities, and economies, and to engineer their modernization. With African and Africanist sociologists came a succession of conceptual and methodological approaches, ranging from the "acculturation" and "modernization" theses of the pluralists to the materialist and class concerns of the Marxists.

The will-to-knowledge and the will-to-power were locked in a fateful paradigmatic and prescriptive embrace in political science, which wrestled with two fundamental questions: how to construct coherent political communities within the territorial contrivances inherited from colonialism (nation-building) and how to build institutions and technologies for effective governance over the newly forged political communities (state-building). In the 1960s, much of the discourse was guided by the evolutionary hopes of modernization theory. By the 1980s, however, the postcolonial state had fallen from grace, and Africanist political scientists began to recast African politics and states as "crisis-ridden," while competing to coin the most gratuitous epithets for the postcolonial leviathan. The gloom of Afropessimism

The World Bank began to generously fund African university economics departments and consortia that concerned themselves with the intricacies of the neoliberal gospel.

was most pronounced in the Africanist centers of the global North, but it found powerful echoes among some of Africa's own dispirited academics, although many others took strong umbrage to this discourse.

In the meantime, development economics emerged out of neoclassical economics, inheriting its parent's veneration for the "invisible hand" of the market, a belief in the two commandments of perfect competition and perfect rationality, an indifference to the classical concerns of growth and distribution, and a fondness for dualities. Africa and the "Third World" proved a fertile source of dualities: "modern-traditional" societies, "market-subsistence" economies, and "formal-informal" sectors. Marxist economics briefly won adherents in revolutionary states seeking to substitute underdeveloped capitalism with doctrinaire socialism. Also attractive in intellectual circles and the circuits of Third World solidarity and summitry was dependency theory, which emphasized external constraints to development and saw salvation in the vague ideology of self-reliance, with rhetorical agitation for a new international economic order. Both tendencies perished with the collapse of socialism in the 1980s and early 1990s, presaged by the resurgence of the uncompromising tenets of neoliberalism, of market fundamentalism. Before long, development economics largely disappeared from the discipline of economics. The World Bank, seeking to produce a new generation of pliant African economists, began to generously fund African university economics departments and consortia that concerned themselves with the intricacies of the neoliberal gospel.

The culturalist and developmentalist traditions had enjoyed competing and shifting hegemonies in African universities and African studies for many decades. From the turn of the 1970s, however, counterhegemonic insurgencies arose, first centered around radical Marxist and feminist paradigms, and later by the interventions of the more ambiguous "posts": poststructuralism, postmodernism, and, above all, postcolonialism. Collectively, these

Feminism exposed the underlying androcentric biases of all major disciplinary and theoretical narratives, including Marxism.

paradigms constitute what I call the *deconstructionist tradition*, by which I mean to capture the efforts that emerged within African studies to deconstruct prevailing and dominant analyses associated with the culturalist and developmentalist traditions. In a way, of course, postcolonial African studies as a whole, both within and outside the continent, has been deconstructionist, insofar as it has sought to dismantle the Eurocentric epistemic hegemonies that have dominated the study of Africa.

The rise of these deconstructionist conceptual systems can be attributed—as all paradigm shifts can—to changing and complexly interconnected intellectual, institutional, and ideological contexts, both within and outside the academy. The popularity of Marxist analysis in many African institutions and in African studies program abroad grew alongside disenchantment with the limited fruits of the "first independence," and as greater faith was placed in the transformational potential of the radical liberation movements in southern Africa. In the world at large, this was a period of radical politics—from the universities to the United Nations—as previously disaffected constituencies, both students and developing countries, sought to remake the existing institutional and international orders. Marxism brought class analysis to African studies, which demolished the endearing and enduring myths of nationalist historiography and scholarship around a classless, communalistic Africa. Marxism also brought historical and structural analyses of African political economies from the stylized models and dualisms of modernization theories in development economics, political science, and sociology.

The women's movement exploded on the academic and political scene as women demanded greater gender equity—in both parliamentary and paradigmatic representation—for economic and epistemological empowerment. Ironically, the failures of developmentalism, especially rural development, provided a critical impetus to the women's movement in Africa, giving rise to the Women in Development (WID) project, which subsequently mutated into Women and Development (WAD) and Gender and Development (GAD). The women's development project, together with more radical feminist perspectives, including African critiques of white, Western academic feminism, provided a fertile ground for feminist scholarly production. Feminism exposed the underlying androcentric biases of all major disciplinary and theoretical narratives, including Marxism. Feminist scholars embarked on a vigorous mission to incorporate women's studies in and to genderize African studies.

• • •

THE 1980s USHERED in a new moment in intellectual and international politics and the global economic order. In Euroamerica, there was a sharp turn to the right following the rise to power of conservative governments in the major countries, beginning with Thatcher's Britain, Reagan's America, Mulroney's Canada, and Kohl's Germany. In the meantime, the Soviet Union and its allies accelerated toward implosion, and China rediscovered the virtues of capitalism. Global systemic options narrowed as neoliberalism assumed ascendancy. And our beloved Africa, battered by declining economic growth rates and SAPs, basically lost the 1980s and 1990s, engulfed as it was by the convulsions of struggles for the "second independence." It was an inauspicious time for radical ideologies such as revolutionary feminism, Marxism, and dependency theories, which all but perished in the collapse of socialism in the 1980s and early 1990s.

Postcolonialism has stressed the importance of reverse flows, and of bidirectional flows.

The various "posts" emerged in this context, including postcolonialism, which has been particularly attractive to literary scholars, recovering anthropologists, and qualitative sociologists. It has given greater succor among Africanists in the global North than in Africa and, within Africa itself, more among Francophone and South African scholars than elsewhere on the continent. Postcolonialism has helped to open up and refine important themes, topics, and trends that were previously ignored or undertheorized. In African historical studies, for example, it has recast the nature of metropolitan-colonial connections. Whereas, before, the tendency was to see a unidirectional metropolitan-colonial connection emphasizing the flow of ideas, influences, institutions, and even individuals from the metropole to the colony, postcolonialism has stressed the importance of reverse flows, and of bidirectional flows. After all, the "metropole" was itself as much a creation of the imperial project as were the colonies. Europe and Africa, whiteness and blackness, were mutually constituted.

We are now much more aware of the role of colonial discourse as an incarnation and instrument of power. We better understand the discursive processes through which ideas and images of the colonized and colonizer were created, how the very notion of "Africa" was invented—as Mudimbe has demonstrated in his magisterial tomes, *The Invention of Africa* (1988) and *The Idea of Africa* (1994)—through the conceptual registers of the new academic disciplines and the disciplining ideologies of missionary Christianity and the institutions of colonial education. We see how hierarchies of difference and African alterity were produced and reproduced through the temporal, spatial, and social teleologies and epistemic violence of Eurocentric history, geography, anthropology, linguistics, and philosophy. We see now how power was located, acted out, and fought over in specific institutions and contexts by various social groups and projects.

Since 1990, more attention has been paid to everyday forms of resistance and the discourses among the various subaltern groups, including the youth.

Postcolonial analyses of the dynamics of reproduction have also generated important insights into the social reproduction of the colonial order, enriching Marxism-inspired studies on labor reproduction and feminist research on women's productive and reproductive roles in colonial society (revealing that women subsidize migrant labor and the colonial economy as a whole, despite their marginalization). Studies of what can be called "intimate colonialism" have sharpened the focus on sexuality, the shifting constructions of gender and racial identities, and colonial representations of African sexuality, the control of which was central to ideologies of colonial domination. Postcolonial studies have looked at how different masculinities—dominant and hegemonic, subordinate and subversive—were produced and performed in different class, racial, institutional, and spatial contexts, and how they changed over time.

Studies of anticolonial resistance—previously preoccupied with social content and composition and the continuities and discontinuities marked by decolonization—have also been reconfigured. By the 1980s, the old accounts of elite politics and heroic resistance had largely been abandoned in favor of analyses of resistance by peasants, workers, and women. Since 1990, more attention has been paid to everyday forms of resistance and the discourses among the various subaltern groups, including the youth. Some historians embraced the perspectives of the Indian Subaltern Studies group and their notion of "alternative nationalisms" among peasants, which took seriously peasant action and intellectual production.

Despite these contributions, many African scholars, particularly those at African universities, harbor deep misgivings about postcolonialism. They caution against the abandonment of categories that were critical to earlier analytical and revolutionary discourses—especially *nation* and *class*, and the mischievous celebration of hybridity and borderlands—which encourage the sanitization and depiction of imperialism and colonialism as "shared" cultures, negotiated discursive spaces. Valorization of colonial ambivalence and hybridity ignores the fact that colonialism was a space and moment that entailed not only negotiations, but also negations. The specificities of African subjectification and the persistent imaginings of national liberation were, and continue to be,

Can African studies escape— even transcend—the Eurocentric coding, the seductions and sanctions of writing Africa by analogy?

written in pain and suffering, sweat and blood. The multiplication of identities, memories, and resistances surely must not be used to forget the larger contexts: the hierarchies of power between the colonizer and the colonized, Europe and Africa; the unequal impact the empire had and left behind for the metropoles and the colonies; the fact that imperial power was upheld by physical force (not simply by ideas and images); and that it was underpinned by material structures (not simply ideological constructs), and by political economy (not simply discursive economy).

The erasures of revolution, nation, class, history, and reality, even if they may have started as critiques, turn the "posts" into legitimating ideologies of contemporary global configurations of power and production. Insofar as capitalism is not as fragmented as it is often assumed to be, the "posts" bolster the capitalist order itself by becoming a part of the ideological apparatus that sustains the inability of exploited nations and social classes—splintered in their various cultural identities—to mobilize counterhegemonically. The analytical power of postcolonial theory will remain limited unless it tempers its facile celebration of newness, cosmopolitanism, and globalization in a world reeling from endless war and deepening inequalities, and places its favorite tropes of disjuncture and disorder in the context of the enhanced regulatory power of contemporary global capitalism. It must reconnect culture to political economy, pay attention to both localized or

Kwaku,
Wawa Aba
(Perseverance).
2006. Mixed
media, 53 x
75 inches

microstruggles and broad anti-imperialist struggles, and consider how capitalist adjustments are reinstating and restructuring gender identities. Postcolonial theory must restore focus on nationalism, because the nation-state constitutes the site through which hegemonic capitalism operates and against which resistance can be organized.

The globalist tradition is rooted in Eurocentrism, which is inherently comparative and universalistic in its intellectual gaze and ambitions. Since the establishment of the modern academy in Europe, African phenomena have always been measured according to European master references—from humanity to history, civilization to culture, ethics to economics, temporalities to technologies, sociality to sexuality—and always found lacking, lagging behind Europe. But the African response, too, even in its militant Afrocentric forms, has largely consisted of investing Africa with the imagined positive attributes of Europe, rather than dismantling the very foundations of this colonizing epistemological order. Can African studies escape—even transcend—the Eurocentric coding, the seductions and sanctions of writing Africa by analogy?

In globalization discourses Africa is sometimes, strangely enough, seen as marginal to globalization, when it has in fact been central to the construction of the modern world, with all its ramifications—economic, political, cultural, and discursive—over the half-millennium since the emergence of the Atlantic world system. As Samir Amin has forcefully argued, Africa's so-called marginalization—on the one hand, the continent, or much of it, is out of the global system or integrated into it only superficially; on the other, the poverty of African peoples is precisely the result of their not being sufficiently integrated into the global system—is not borne out by the facts. Stripped of globaloney, globalization is both an ideological project of neo-liberal capitalist restructuring and a long-term historical process of interconnectedness. African scholars have not contributed much to such globalization literature and debates. More productive, in my view, has been the globalist tradition arising out of diaspora studies.

•   •   •

THE GROWTH OF African interest in the diaspora is partly fueled by the rising emigration of highly educated Africans to the global North. For example, according to the 2000 U.S. Census, among African-born U.S. residents aged twenty-five years and above, 49.3 percent had a bachelor's degree or more, as compared to 25.6 percent for the native-born population and 25.8 percent for the foreign-born population as a whole. The new diaspora is coveted by African governments for its social capital—skills, knowledge, networks, civic awareness, cultural experience, and cosmopolitanism—that can not only provide access to global markets and investment but also stimulate technological innovation. The new diaspora is also Africa's biggest donor—according to World Bank estimates, in 2006, the new diaspora remitted $39 billion; other estimates are as large as $150 billion. Not surprisingly, governments increasingly regard the diaspora as a critical remittance pipeline, an important economic asset.

The African diaspora studies movement represents a return to the future of the Pan-Africanist scholarship of Edward Blyden and W. E. B. Du Bois, who always tried to understand and situate Africa into worldly representation and recognition, to affirm an African presence that was both unique and equal to others. Diaspora studies offer a key avenue for globalizing African history and contesting European appropriations of global history, enabling us to rewrite the histories of the various regions to which Africans were dispersed, whether voluntarily or by force. The Africans who conquered and ruled parts of the Iberian Peninsula between 711 and 1492 CE, establishing what the Moroccan scholar Anouar Majid calls an "African kingdom in Europe," did so voluntarily, while those who were shipped to the Americas during the Atlantic slave trade were coerced. Both left an indelible mark on the history of Europe, Africa, and the Americas, whose effects are still with us and are central to understanding the history of the Atlantic world. The same is true of the Indian Ocean world, whose history cannot be fully grasped without the imprint of African activities, migrations, and diasporas. Conversely, the European and Asian diasporas to Africa, and the contemporary Afro-

Eurocentrism seeks to universalize the West and provincialize the rest.

European and Afro-Asian diasporas from Africa, are simultaneously part of African and world histories. Eurocentrism seeks to universalize the West and provincialize the rest, but diaspora studies subvert that imperial self-fashioning and give Africans global historical agency. Interest in diaspora studies among Africanists and African scholars on the continent is growing, which offers the possibility of integrating the various institutional, ideological, and intellectual tendencies of African studies into productive engagement, and the ASA now regularly features themes and topics on the subject. African studies today is a house of many mansions, a field with diverse, complex, and fascinating disciplinary, interdisciplinary, and global dimensions. The days when one country, one center—or one paradigm, for that matter—dominated African studies are long gone. For some, this apparent fragmentation is a source of deep concern; for others, it represents scholarly pluralization and a cause for celebration.

Only when universities on the continent fully recover and take their rightful—and leading—role in the production of African scholarly knowledges will African studies in the rest of the world become a truly strong field. From the late 1990s on, African leaders, educators, researchers, and external donors became increasingly aware of the challenges facing African higher education, and the need for renewal, if the continent was to achieve higher rates of growth and development and compete in an increasingly knowledge-intensive global economy. The reform agenda has centered on five broad sets of issues, although

Critical for Africa is the changing role of external donors, from the philanthropic foundations to the World Bank and other international financial institutions and multilateral agencies.

expressions of concern have yet to be matched by the provision of adequate resources. First, the need to examine systematically the philosophical foundations of African universities is widely recognized. Included in this are the principles underpinning public higher education in an era of privatization: the conception, content, and consequences of the reforms currently being undertaken across the continent, and the public-private interface in African higher education systems. Second, African universities are grappling with the challenges of quality control, funding, and governance in response to the establishment of new regulatory regimes; growing pressures for finding alternative sources of funding; changing demographics and massification; increasing demands for access and equity for underrepresented groups, including women; and the emergence of new forms of student and faculty politics in the face of the democratization of the wider society.

There are also pedagogical and paradigmatic issues, ranging from the languages of instruction in African universities and other educational systems as a whole to the dynamics of knowledge production—the societal relevance of the knowledges produced in African higher education systems and how those knowledges are disseminated and consumed by students, scholarly communities, and the general public.

Another aspect of the reform agenda focuses on the role of universities in the pursuit of the historic project of Africa nationalism: decolonization, development, democratization, nation-building, and regional integration are all under scrutiny. Included here are questions of the uneven and changing relations between universities and the state, civil society, and industry, as well as the role of universities in helping to manage and resolve the various crises that confront the African continent, from civil conflicts to disease epidemics, most notably HIV/AIDS. The role that universities have played and can play in the future to either promote or undermine the pan-African project is also of great interest, as African states, *via* the African Union, renew their efforts to achieve closer integration both within Africa and between Africa and its diasporas.

The new reform agenda also examines the impact of global trends associated with new information and communication technologies, expansion of the transborder or transnational provision of higher education, and the General Agreement on Trade in Services (GATS) regime. Critical for Africa is the changing role of external donors, from the philanthropic foundations to the World Bank and other international financial institutions and multilateral agencies. The impact of these trends on African higher education, and *vice versa*, are of utmost importance and will benefit from fruitful collaboration between researchers from Africa and other world regions.

The challenges facing African universities are serious and disquieting, but higher education in Africa has a long history, dating back to ancient Christian and Islamic institutions of higher learning, and it will have a long future. The onus for ensuring that such a future is a healthy and productive one lies primarily with African leaders, educators, and scholars, who cannot afford the morbid indulgences of Afropessimism, which has so often afflicted Africanists outside the continent. Productive engagement with African institutions and principled commitment to critical and empowering scholarship can provide a useful antidote and help to advance the long-standing agendas of African universities for their own epistemic and institutional decolonization, along with those of African studies everywhere. ▦

Kwaku Ofori-Yirenkyi

Kwaku Ofori-Yirenkyi—also known as *Absku*—describes his art as "a search for a personal and social identity." Kwaku, who was born in Ghana, has lived in the United States since the age of twelve—now more than half of his life. His work ranges over various styles and media, and reflects influences from both his first and second cultures; through immersion and assimilation of the two cultures, a "third" culture is created, which Kwaku describes as "the transformation that an individual goes through when uprooted from the original homeland, the first culture." Kwaku thus bridges his first and second cultures through his work as an artist.

In his diaspora representations, Kwaku uses symbols from Adinkra, a traditional language of Ghanaian origin. The word *Adinkra* means *saying goodbye when parting ways*. These symbols—based on nonfigurative shapes, plant life, human-made objects, the human body, and animals—remind people of proverbs and ideas about life. Kwaku uses the symbols playfully, allowing his paintings to take on their own identities as graphic statements of the many realities and identities in life.

> *I am aware of the plurality of my cultural influences. This awareness increases my interest in expressing that duality in my artwork. I consider my work as an impression and expression of traditional Ghanaian and contemporary Western cultural influences. My work explores the multitudes of identities that result from migration as part of the African diaspora.*

> —Kwaku Ofori-Yirenki

The Geography and Dimensions of Poverty in the Global Economy

historical origins and looming consequences in Planet of Slums (2006), *by Mike Davis*

Joseph E. Inikori

PLANET OF SLUMS (2006), by Mike Davis, belongs to a vast literature focused on factors shaping the long history of humanity on planet Earth in the direction of global conflict over the distribution of world resources among contending groups: classes, races, ethnoreligious groups, nations, etc. Karl Marx and Friedrich Engels focused on conflict over distribution among social classes that was expected to reach its climax in global capitalism, when the highly developed forces of production and the class conflict generated by the social relations of production would pave the way for the establishment of a socialist global order dominated by the workers of the world. Ultimately, Marx and Engels believed, the socialist world order would lead to the establishment of a communist global system—the highest level of human development—replacing conflict with eternal harmony.

Historical reality, however, seems to have moved in the opposite direction. The revolutionary leaders of Russia, after waiting in vain for socialist revolutions in the mature capitalist nations of Western Europe and North America (between 1917 and the 1920s) settled for "Socialism in One Country." Western strategies for the global spread of free market capitalism during the Cold War—fought between the leaders of the capitalist and socialist movements—appear to have succeeded beyond even the expectations of Western political and business leaders. The demonstration effect of the "Asian Miracle" and the collapse of what some characterize as "state capitalism" in Eastern Europe and the U.S.S.R. have forced virtually everyone to embrace the free market model of development. This apparent triumph of capitalism has been celebrated as the end of history: the class conflicts articulated by Marx and Engels have been resolved in favor of the capitalists, contrary to the prognostications of Marx and Engels. Eternal harmony, it is proclaimed, will prevail under global capitalism instead of communism.

Still, a number of scholars continue to believe that the conflicts predicted by Marx and Engels have yet to be resolved. They argue, specifically, that if the conditions that allowed the Asian miracle in the period from 1950 to

"A profound enquiry into an
urgent subject ... a brilliant book."
Arundhati Roy

PLANET
OF SLUMS
MIKE DAVIS

1970 cannot be reproduced for all the imitators, disappointment and the
attendant employment problems will generate conflicts far greater than
those predicted by Marx and Engels. *Planet of Slums* offers empirical details
and historical analysis to drive home this argument.

Before the "Asian miracle" was successfully marketed as the panacea
for economic backwardness in the less-developed regions of the world,
concerned world leaders did not see distribution of world resources among
classes as a potential source of global conflict, as Marx and Engels had.
Instead, regional distribution—especially North-South distribution—was
expected to be the main source of strife. Thus, Willy Brandt, the chairman
of an independent commission (the Willy Brandt Commission) established
in 1977 to study and suggest solutions to the problem of North-South distribution, observed in the Commission's report:

> When we first met near Bonn in December 1977, we
> regarded it as our task (as we said in our terms of reference)
> "to study the grave global issues arising from the economic
> and social disparities of the world community." . . . When

we came to discuss our conclusions, there was an even stronger feeling that reshaping worldwide North-South relations had become a crucial commitment to the future of mankind. Equal in importance to counteracting the dangers of the arms race, we believed this to be the greatest challenge to mankind for the remainder of this century.

Planet of Slums reaffirms both the class conflict articulated by Marx and Engels and the looming North-South clash prophesied by Willy Brandt. While the Brandt Commission presented the clash in purely regional terms, Mike Davis presents the North-South clash itself in class terms. His evidence and analysis show a geographical shift of poverty over time—from the inner cities of the developed industrial nations to the countrysides of less-developed countries and, finally, to the cities of the latter countries. The concentration of global poverty in the cities of less-developed countries has created a global reality in which the main source of global conflict is class specific—*per* Marx and Engels—and at the same time region specific—*per* the Brandt Commission.

. . .

TO ENABLE US to appreciate the magnitude of the problem addressed by Davis, a brief summary of his evidence is needed. The evidence points to rapid urban population growth worldwide as the volcanic center of the problem. In 1950, cities with 1 million people and above numbered 86 worldwide; by 2005, the number had increased to 400, with 550 as the projection for the year 2015. Cities, with a total population of 3.2 billion in 2005, have absorbed almost two-thirds of "the global population explosion since 1950." The global countryside no longer absorbs more people, and its population will begin to decrease in absolute terms by 2020. What is particularly significant, the bulk of the global urban population growth has occurred in less-developed countries, where 95 percent of the projected growth will be located. A few Third World cities taken from Davis's table are illustrative in this regard. The population of Mexico City grew from 2.9 million in 1950 to 22.1 million in 2004; Bombay (India), from 2.9 million to 19.1 million; Lagos (Nigeria), from 0.3 million to 13.4 million. These explosive increases may be compared with New York City, whose population grew from 12.3 million to 21.9 million during the same period. As Davis tells us,

The main source of global conflict is class specific—*per* Marx and Engels—and at the same time region specific—*per* the Brandt Commission.

following this phenomenon of Third World urban growth, 80 percent of Marx's industrial proletariat now resides outside Western Europe and the United States.

Davis's evidence shows that the rapid growth of urban population in the less-developed countries has proceeded *pari passu* with the growth of poverty generally, but slums have grown even more in those cities. Taking slums as geographical concentrations of abject poverty in cities, Davis nevertheless cautions that urban poverty is not limited to slums, and not all slum dwellers are poor. Still, there is no escaping the fact that, in general, slums exhibit conditions of extreme poverty. As Davis notes, even the understated U.N. figures show 921 million slum dwellers worldwide in 2001; the figure rose to more than 1 billion by 2005. Significantly, while only 6 percent of the city populations of the developed countries are slum dwellers, residents of slums "constitute a staggering 78.2 percent of urbanites in the least developed countries . . . fully a third of the global urban population." In general, the living conditions of these Third World slum residents are deplorable: overcrowding, poor housing and sanitation, inadequate access to safe water and healthcare, and poor urban transportation. Differential infant mortality rates sum up the conditions: 151 per 1000 in Nairobi's slums, "two or three times higher than in the city as a whole and half again as high as in poor rural areas."

Eighty percent of Marx's industrial proletariat now resides outside Western Europe and the United States.

•   •   •

WHAT HISTORICAL PROCESSES gave rise to the current situation, and what trends are observable? Here, Davis's account leaves out some of the critical elements. He focuses correctly on Third World state policies based on neoliberal orthodoxy as defined by the International Monetary Fund (IMF) and the World Bank—the operation of market forces without state intervention. But Davis does not accurately account for the creation of the conditions which brought these financial institutions into policymaking in the Third World, and the forces that have influenced their policy recommendations. This partly explains some of the contradictions in Davis's analysis. For example, Davis argues that "the Third World now contains many examples of capital-intensive" agriculture, which pushes people from the countryside to cities crippled industrially by IMF and World Bank policies. But, in sub-Saharan Africa, he says, rapid urbanization takes place without capital-intensive agriculture—without "rising agricultural productivity."

Clearly, the historical process was not the same in the sub-regions of the Third World. In Latin America, a critical element was the creation of politically powerful, large landholders over the several centuries from the colonial period to the agricultural export booms of the nineteenth century. Several economic historians have explained the failure of politically independent Latin American countries to vigorously pursue industrialization in the nineteenth century—having opted instead for free trade, specifically, the export of primary products in exchange for imported manufactures—in terms of the self-interests of the large landholders and their allies. When the devastating impact of the two World Wars and the Great Depression compelled import substitution industrialization in the twentieth century,

In Latin America, a critical element was the creation of politically powerful, large landholders.

the agrarian structure, characterized by the prevalence of *latifundias/haciendas* (very large landholdings) and *minifundias* (very small holdings), was one of the major factors which made it impossible even for countries with great potential, such as Brazil, Argentina, and Mexico, to successfully complete the industrialization process. The lopsided agrarian structure gave rise to underutilization of resources (both land and labor), thus reducing the capacity of the countryside to operate as a virile market for the products of urban industry. While constraining the growth of urban industrial employment, the agrarian structure which limited access to land by the vast majority of the rural population operated at the same time as a powerful push factor forcing millions to the cities. Government efforts to apply corrective measures through land reforms were frustrated by large landholders in alliance with both the military and the agents of U.S. capital.

In sub-Saharan Africa, Cold War–induced civil wars played some role, as Davis explains. But, in Nigeria, the oil boom of the 1970s and early 1980s first triggered the process. Characteristic of what is now called "Dutch disease," the spread effects of the growth of income from oil pulled resources from all sectors *except* oil and trade. Overvalued currency encouraged imports and discouraged investment in domestic production, including industry and agriculture. The importation of subsidized rice from the United States by the Shagari administration undermined rice production in northern Nigeria. Ultimately, the importation and distribution of imported goods became the main source of wealth, second only to lucrative government appointments with access to oil money. Belated efforts to control imports through import license and foreign exchange management only offered opportunities for official corruption, coordinated by Western business gurus who sowed the seeds of what is now known in Nigeria as "419 (scam)." If one knows how many billions of dollars these gurus (exemplified by the notorious American Marc Rich) looted from Nigeria, one can understand the anger of many Nigerians when the Western media complain about the so-called Nigerian scam without saying a word about the billions looted from the country by "respected" Western entrepreneurs. (It recalls a line from Bernard Shaw's 1903 play, "Man and Superman": "I am a brigand: I live by robbing the rich. I am a gentleman: I live by robbing the poor. Shake hands.") For Nigeria, at least, this was the initial process leading to what Davis refers to as urbanization without industrialization and without rising agricultural productivity. This process also gave rise to an important development not mentioned by Davis. The ecological impact of oil production destroyed the means of livelihood for millions of people in the Niger Delta, without the government or the multinational oil companies providing any alternative. It is difficult to say whether poverty in Ajegunle (a Lagos slum) is any worse than what we have become accustomed to seeing on television in the Niger Delta.

As for the role of the IMF and the World Bank, Davis's account is incomplete and/or inaccurate in places. Contrary to the impression created by Davis, the coercive power wielded by these financial institutions, collectively owned by the taxpayers of the world, is not directly connected to the magnitude of the loans they have granted to Third World nations. Their power comes, instead, from their governing role in the global financial market, which allows them to operate as "medical doctors" testifying to the financial health—credit worthiness—of national economies. The willingness of the IMF and the World Bank to grant what amounts to, in most

The Western media complain about the so-called Nigerian scam without saying a word about the billions looted from the country by "respected" Western entrepreneurs.

cases, token loans to a country signals to the global financial corporations that the country is financially healthy (in other words, the country's economic policies have the institutions' seal of approval). Without that signal, countries owing huge external debts to global financial corporations cannot operate in the global financial market, meaning that they must pay cash for everything they need from the global market.

Thus, to get the narrative right, we need to move the entry of the IMF and the World Bank to a later period in the story. The narrative should start with the huge windfalls accumulated suddenly by the members of OPEC (Organization of Petroleum Exporting Countries) following multiple increases in oil prices in the 1970s. Unable to absorb much of the windfall at home, OPEC nations deposited their petro-dollars in Western banks. To be able to pay the normal interests on these deposits, Western banks had to look for borrowers, whom they found in Third World countries (especially Latin America), where governments engaged in long-term development processes were enticed by loan-pushing banks to accumulate external debts, usually on floating interest rates. The recklessness with which these loans were granted was very similar to the recent irresponsible mortgage lending in the United States. The global financial crisis that followed in the 1980s and continued thereafter was also similar. It was after the crisis erupted that the IMF and the World Bank stepped in.

The heavily indebted Third World countries found their economies in a situation very similar to that of the developed industrial economies of the West at the end of World War II: inadequate aggregate demand led to underemployment of resources, both capacity underutilization and labor unemployment. Those conditions inspired Keynesian economics and the founding of IMF and the World Bank. Hence, the policy focus of these institutions at that time was expansionary: stimulate aggregate demand in order to bring about growth and employment. And this was done through the active cooperation of governments and the market.

One might have expected the IMF and the World Bank to deal with the Third World problem in the same way. This did not happen. On the contrary, these governing institutions of the global financial market forced contractionary policies on these countries and enthroned what a Nobel Prize economist, Joseph Stiglitz, calls *market fundamentalism*: total reliance on the market, with governments doing virtually nothing. These policies have been very damaging to the industrialization process in Third World countries, thereby creating unemployment problems in their cities, Davis correctly argues. Scholars have struggled to understand why the policies imposed by the IMF and the World Bank on indebted Third World countries in the 1980s and 1990s were so different from those implemented in the immediate post–World War II period.

The most persuasive explanation has been offered by Stiglitz, a chief economist and senior vice-president of the World Bank from 1997 to 2000. According to Stiglitz, the institutions moved away from their Keynesian foundation as a result of two important developments. The first was their reorganization by U.S. President Ronald Reagan and U.K. Prime Minister Margaret Thatcher in the early 1980s. The second was the effective extension of the vested self-interests of the global financial corporations to the two governing institutions.

The ecological impact of oil production destroyed the means of livelihood for millions of people in the Niger Delta.

The consequence of these developments was that the self-interests of the financial corporations came to take precedence over the long-term development needs of the less-developed countries in the formulation of policy by the IMF and the World Bank. Thus, the conditionalities and structural adjustment programs were intended first and foremost to serve the interests of commercial banks in getting Third World countries to pay their debts. The long-term development needs of these countries were not seriously considered. The conditionalities and adjustment programs did not produce growth and employment. They produced unemployment and misery in the Third World, while making resources available to service the external debts. In other words, these institutions operated as debt collectors for the commercial banks.

· · ·

WHILE DAVIS'S HISTORICAL explanations are incomplete and inaccurate in places, his account of the consequences of the policy prescriptions of the IMF and the World Bank is no exaggeration. His argument, that the growth of the "informal economy"—street vendors and other informal entrepreneurs—is the product of the survival strategies of the unemployed slum residents, is both fascinating and accurate. So, too, is his account of the desperate efforts of the elite in Third World, slum-ridden cities to protect themselves from the swelling wave of crime, as devastating poverty forces people to do desperate things. One is reminded of a statement by a Nigerian economist, Professor Sam Aluko: "The poor people in Nigeria cannot sleep, because they are hungry, and the rich people cannot sleep, because the poor people are awake." The looming global crisis predicted is ominous. Davis puts it in the words of a like mind:

> As Jan Breman, writing of India, has warned: "A point of no return is reached when a reserve army waiting to be incorporated into the labour process becomes stigmatized as a permanently redundant mass, an excessive burden that cannot be included now or in the future, in economy and society. This metamorphosis is, in my opinion at least, the real crisis of world capitalism."

One may not agree with everything Davis says in *Planet of Slums*, but readers will agree that this is an engaging book, focused seriously and elaborately on a major issue concerning the future of our "global village."

Black French Intellectualism and the Rise of Afro-European Studies

a review of Pap Ndiaye's La condition noire: Essai sur une minorité française *(2008)*

Safoi Babana-Hampton

PAP NDIAYE, a French historian of Senegalese origin and professor of the social sciences at the École des Hautes Études in Paris, opens *La condition noire* [*The Black Condition*] anecdotally, with a short story by Marie Ndiaye, his sister and a well-known writer. The short story allegorically presents the various ways that "blacks" in France, understood as individuals and groups of African or Antillean origin, come to terms with their experience of being an "invisible" minority. Ndiaye profitably calls our attention to the paucity in the French social sciences of serious scholarship that focuses on the condition of blacks as a French *minority* (rather than being considered abstractly as a *community* or *people*) in contemporary metropolitan France. Ndiaye explains that by the "condition" of blacks, he means a social situation that characterizes the life of a minority whose members have in common the experience of being regarded as black.

Ndiaye provides a well-documented historical account of the shortcomings of the social sciences in France. His study not only examines the perceived failure of the French social sciences to effectively render an account of the phenomenon of "racial discrimination" in France, but also challenges the very civic organisms and antidiscrimination associations—such as SOS Racisme—that have been visibly dedicated to fighting discrimination since the 1980s. In both cases, Ndiaye sees a failure to address, for obviously different reasons, the important question of *structural racism*, which significantly shapes a whole way of living and thinking in French society. While the French social sciences, in Ndiaye's view, simply reject "race" as an analytical category and perpetuate in this manner the invisibility of blacks, SOS Racisme and similar groups address only *acts* of racism (such as verbal or physical aggression), instead of calling into question the structures of thinking that promote, in a much broader way, the occurrence of such social phenomena.

By his own admission, Ndiaye writes from the double position of a researcher who unapologetically uses the theoretical and methodological models of the Anglo-American social sciences, and an active member of

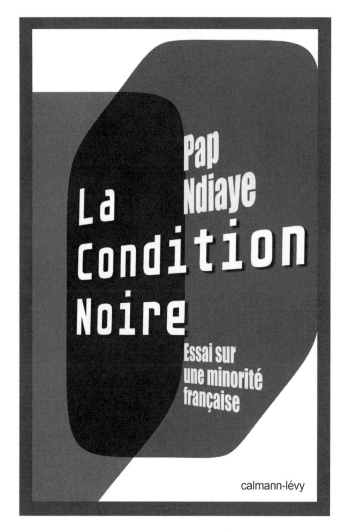

local civic associations that promote social equality for the blacks of France. On the one hand, as an Americanist, Ndiaye investigates the "racial question" in France; firmly believing in the theoretical and practical merits of Anglo-American models, he maintains that "*le comparativisme est essentiel sur les questions relatives aux minorités raciales* [comparativism is essential to questions pertaining to the racial minorities]." On the other hand, Ndiaye positions himself as a member of both the Cercle d'Action pour la Promotion de la Diversité en France (CAPDIV) [Action Circle for the Promotion of Diversity in France] and the Conseil Représentatif des Associations Noires (CRAN) [Representative Council for the Black Associations of France]. His position as both comparativist observer and civic activist mirrors and informs Ndiaye's complex approach to the subject, and he firmly asserts that new insights and a better understanding of the black condition can emerge only through historical and cross-cultural perspectives. In his view, we should steer the discussion toward perceptions of the notion of "race," not in objectivist, essentialist terms, but as essentially locked up in historically situated and socially determined power relations.

In a crisp and particularly lucid style, Ndiaye meticulously outlines his approach within the framework of the Anglo-American model of postcolonial theory and cultural studies, while at the same time consciously dealing with and attempting to transcend their limitations. Citing a wide range of intellectuals and writers who have influenced postcolonial theory—Frantz Fanon, Aimé Césaire, James Baldwin, Anthony Appiah, and Paul Gilroy, among others—Ndiaye argues that his study, inspired by the Anglo-American experience, is a call for the development of new approaches to the black condition in France.

Of special interest is Ndiaye's analysis of the limitations of the two dominant approaches to the black condition: the first rejects *race* as a category and adopts purely sociological parameters that betray economic determinism; the second, in contrast, privileges the category of *race*, which inevitably yields essentialist worldviews and strips treatments of the black condition of its politically, socially, and historically specific dimensions.

"*Être noir* [being black]" is neither an essence nor a culture but a product of social relations.

Ndiaye continuously asserts his deep awareness of the problematic nature of the notion of *race* in social analysis and its impact on perceptions of the black condition. Nevertheless, he aims to deliver the tools needed to move beyond the two opposed and mutually exclusive alternatives: on the one hand, by adopting a "minority approach" that attends to the *external* as well as the *internal* frontiers that define the French national identity; and, on the other hand, by incorporating the notion of *race* as an essentially historical and social construct that represents one among many variables and modalities of social relations, which are in turn caught up in power relations. Ndiaye places race on an equal footing with other, related categories, such as gender, class, and nation.

In chapter one, "*Le fait d'être noir* [The Fact of Being Black]," the title of which unmistakably echoes Frantz Fanon's well-known "*L'expérience vécue du noir* [The lived experience of the black]," Ndiaye presents a subjective account of the experience of blacks—specifically, their sense of being "invisible" and "outsiders." More importantly, this chapter offers a structural analysis of intersubjective relations and identity positions constituted within a specific system of social relations in which black persons' French-ness is contested or rejected. Here, Ndiaye invokes the results of field investigations to support the claim that many blacks today affirm their plural identities as the very essence of their French-ness.

The next chapter, "*Gens de couleur* [People of Color]," further develops the ideological and methodological implications of the prevailing theoretical models in the French social sciences. This is done by discussing the premise that "*être noir* [being black]" is neither an essence nor a culture but a product of social relations. By taking a critical look at various attitudes among blacks in France toward the question of "color," and by drawing illuminating parallels to those of African Americans and British blacks, Ndiaye suggests that while *être noir* in the "French black minority" presents itself as a real concern and persisting preoccupation, "*être blanc* [being white]" passes for an evident fact, so much so that it rarely occurs to one to question, or even mention it.

In "*Vers une histoire des populations noires de France* [Toward a History of the Black Populations of France]," Ndiaye offers a new historical account of black populations in France, which challenges and deconstructs simplistic views that reduce blacks' history to that of slavery, while also addressing the flaws of the French social sciences that exclude the notion of "race" from analysis. He shows how the separation of national history from colonial history is but one of many crippling methodological problems generated by the traditional research practices within the French social sciences. One distinction between national and colonial history rests upon the assimilationist republican model and its abstract conception of *citizenship* as the only valid frame of reference for describing and thinking about the social realities of blacks in France. According to Ndiaye, this leads not only to an evasion of issues such as social inequalities rooted in racial hierarchies, which are, in turn, a product of past colonial ideology, but also to the rise of "laws of inhospitality" toward the blacks of France. This chapter usefully presents the case of the famous "*tirailleurs sénégalais* [Senegalese soldiers]" to subversively situate the account within a perspective of France's colonial history that complicates and problematizes France's national history: "*Le corps des tirailleurs avait été créé par Louis Faidherbe, gouverneur du Sénégal, en 1857, afin de faciliter la colonization française en Afrique noire* [The Senagalese corps was established by Louis Faidherbe, the leader of Senegal, in 1857, in order to facilitate the French colonization of Black Africa]."

The separation of national history from colonial history is but one of many crippling methodological problems.

Chapter four, "*Le tirailleur et le sauvageon* [The Senegalese soldier and the little savage]," shows how negative images and racial perceptions of the body of the *tirailleur sénégalais* continue to inspire contemporary forms of racism and build a repertoire of various forms of symbolic violence, such as can be seen in the domains of culture and sports.

"*Penser les discriminations noires* [Conceptualizing Discrimination against Blacks]," explains why framing the "black question" in terms of "racial discrimination," rather than "racism," yields a deeper understanding of the black condition. This approach stresses the intersubjective nature of the situation of blacks and engages the voices of members of this minority group within a larger framework focusing on the shift in praxis from antidiscrimination *struggles* toward a *politics* of antidiscrimination.

In the final chapter, "*La cause noire* [The Black Cause]," Ndiaye offers a succinct historical account of various forms of solidarity that emerged within the black community in France as far back as 1919 (with the Pan-African Congress held in Paris), bringing together Antillean, African, and African American writers and thinkers. The chapter also takes a look at the *Négritude* movement led by the elite of the French black diaspora, as well as the movement that formed around the militant journal *Présence africaine* (founded in 1947), in addition to numerous migrant associations. Ndiaye attempts in this chapter to answer the question whether various forms of black solidarity can contribute to a better world for all people, not only for blacks. Characteristically taking his cue from the U.S. and, more particularly, the NAACP experience, Ndiaye suggests that a "*politique minoritaire* [minority politics]" promoted by the creation of an interassociative network, bringing together various minority groups and encouraging the defense of their common interests, is the best strategy for effecting a metamorphosis within French politics.

· · ·

NDIAYE DEMONSTRATES A noteworthy ability to investigate what he perceives to be (within France) a nascent field of research, "African European Studies" or "black studies *à la française*," in great depth, using an analytical model that takes into account the complexity of the discipline's own location, at the crossroads of sociology, anthropology, psychoanalysis, history, cultural studies, and postcolonial studies. By drawing on a variety of theoretical perspectives and citing key figures of postcolonial theory in the Anglo-American world, Ndiaye illuminates how a category banished from French scientific discourse—particularly after the racial laws promulgated by and associated with the Vichy regime and Nazi ideology, which rationalized genocidal practices (discussed in chapters one and two)—still lives on in the French imaginary, producing social inequalities that translate into racial hierarchies.

Ndiaye takes aim at the prevailing French Jacobin republican model and its confused position *vis-à-vis* the notion of *race*. On the one hand, the rejection of race as a category for describing the experience of blacks in France is rooted in a general will to denounce a model of social organization associated with the Vichy regime. On the other hand, the republican model is forced to grapple with the moral, social, and scientific consequences (especially the invisibility of blacks in political discourse and scientific research) of eliminating this notion from debates on the condition of blacks in France. Although his main aim is to describe and analyze

A category banished from French scientific discourse still lives on in the French imaginary, producing social inequalities that translate into racial hierarchies.

the present condition of the blacks of France, Ndiaye presents a wealth of perspectives and marshals the main arguments in favor of re-introducing *race* in social and cultural analysis within key historical moments that shaped the lives of the blacks of France (most notably slavery, colonialism, the two World Wars, departmentalization, and immigration). At the same time, he takes issue with historiographical practices that reduce the history of blacks to that of slavery or racism, and the related problem of constructing "French blacks" as a monolithic group. Ndiaye's goal is to *describe* the social experience of the black minority, rather than *prescribe* antidiscrimination public policies.

• • •

NDIAYE'S STUDY APPEARS at an important historical juncture. More than ever before, blacks living in France today are making themselves heard in the national public space, to the extent that it would be perfectly legitimate to talk about an invention of the "black question" in these circles. This rising phenomenon is directly tied to two recent and structurally significant political developments which served as catalysts: the 150th anniversary of the abolition of slavery in 1998, and the adoption of a law in May 2001 recognizing slavery as a crime against humanity. Ndiaye contends that, despite the magnitude of these political events, an important disparity still exists between the social, political, and media presence of the "black question" and the scholarly enterprises that attempt to structure it intellectually.

La condition noire is a compelling study that should be of great interest to Anglo-American readers, students, and scholars interested in postcolonial francophone studies, a field of research within which serious interrogations of the French Jacobin and assimilationist model, and its consequences on the social, artistic, cultural, and political experiences of French minorities of immigrant origin, have been formulated and pursued for several years now. Of equal importance to this ongoing debate is the fact that *La condition noire* is a highly original contribution to current methodological debates within postcolonial francophone studies: the work convincingly makes the case for charting new scholarly directions to bridge a long-existing and awkward intellectual gap between Anglo-American postcolonial studies and French and francophone studies, an issue addressed in recent years by Charles Forsdick, Adlai Murdoch, and others.

More than ever before, blacks living in France today are making themselves heard in the national public space.

Ndiaye's study is one among other expressions in France of a current interest among "black professionals" in using the notion of race in social debate about French minorities. Indeed, terms such as the *black condition*, the *black question*, and the *black cause* have enjoyed a steadily increasing circulation among the "French black minority." In a recent article in the French daily *Le Monde*, Louis-Georges Tin, a French professor of Martinican origin, who is, like Ndiaye, a civic activist and member of Conseil Représentatif des Associations Noires (CRAN), identifies the "black question" in France as a topic that has been neglected by both racist and antiracist movements. Tin, like Ndiaye, maintains that "the black question" can be best examined by seeking inspiration from the Anglo-American experience, especially African Americans' approach to fighting discrimination.

Ms. Stovall's Canticles

*glimpses of the sacred and chillin' art of **Suesan Stovall***

Jeffery McNary

NEW ENGLAND IS hardly known for an absence of culture or a failure among its populace to appreciate the arts. In fact, Cambridge, Massachusetts, can legitimately be tagged as the epicenter, the cradle of the tension and brawls between the cultural milieus of tradition and modernity. Sparks fly from these collisions and engagements on a daily, if not hourly, basis.

The work of Suesan Stovall, recently exhibited in the Neil L. and Angelica Zander Rudenstine Gallery of the W. E. B. Du Bois Institute for African and African American Research at Harvard University, is an example of such an encounter. In this citadel, Ms. Stovall has fronted and framed her song and stories, and in the house that Henry Louis "Skip" Gates, Jr., built, her images—both stinging and sacred—float in the ether as if she's held a backstage pass to the African American experience. Stovall's pieces are neither burdened nor ponderous, yet insisting of some place somewhere, like a talisman, and found in all American households.

The installation "Journey of My Soul: Come Along for the Ride" is a sweeping recount of historical attitudes, and is consistent with Ms. Stovall's interest in assemblage as a medium, and her passionate belief and life journey to discover and develop things not always rolled out along the lines of the obvious.

While studying theater in London, the *complete artist*—an operative in both the visual and performance genres—wandered through markets filled with old wooden chests and boxes and texts and daguerreotypes. There is knowledge and wisdom and magic in such places. There are tales and legends and mythical things. And Suesan Stovall became awed and nudged to create from legacies tossed aside. This she has done with both caresses and curses.

Altar, a multipiece phenomenon which stood at the entrance to the exhibit, strands the memory and imagination of both the viewer and the artist through materials used with delicacy and close attention to color scheme. The introductory wall-mounted work begins with an aged photograph of what appears to be a black woman outside a log cabin with several children, all lined up according to size. An orange pinwheel design stands sunlike above and to their right. The centerpiece presents seven candles arching along the floor, thinly shrouding bowls of beans, along with burnished gold and red rose

Suesan Stovall, *Altar*. 2008. Ancestral installation including sacred objects, African talismans, candles, holy water jawbones and graveyard dirt

petals and gain; oils and ointments line the space behind the makeshift offering, with statuettes and small bottles bearing labels such as *jinx remover*. Feathers and an animal jawbone activate the piece, along with flowers and more small bottles. The final section offers a cerulean blue background with a silver metallic angel figure, its lettering inviting the viewer to knock on "heaven's door."

Ms. Stovall says the work is

> an homage to the Great Spirit, the ancestors, and the creative forces in the universe. The objects in and around it, some coming all the way from Africa, are offerings to the powers that be. Offerings in request of divine protection, guidance, and prayers for abundant life. Not bound by the confines of religion, societal rules and dogma. Just a place to take in some magic and enjoy the feeling.

Both *Coon Song* and *Nigger Blues* represent "teachable moments," by engaging in a visual dialogue. Ms. Stovall refers to these pieces as "explorations of minstrelsy." There is no amnesia involved here. And no lessons layered in abstract. Both works present close-up reminders of violation. Pulsing blacks and reds weep from *Coon Song*, and the beige and tans of *Nigger Blues* interlock

Suesan Stovall, *Altar* (close up). 2008. Ancestral installation including sacred objects, African talismans, candles, holy water jawbones and graveyard dirt

lynching and Uncle Remus on a background of sky blue. Here the artist refuses to take an easy way out. Herself of mixed race, Suesan Stovall was "both deeply disturbed and fascinated by the popularity of an art form that so blatantly degraded African American people" and "found it disturbing that white people in black face singing 'darky songs' was accepted by both black and white people as a form of entertainment."

Deeper into the exhibition we hit an imaginative *habeas corpus* in *Political Correctness*, a composition which came to be as Ms. Stovall was working with her collection of antique stereo viewers. Here, the blacks and whites roll in aboard the tans which outline if not dominate the show, as the artist explains:

> I had two cards, printed different years, with the same image of a typical African market scene, with scenic views of people selling their wares and vegetables, etc. On the back of the first printing was a written description of the scene. The Africans were described as not being far removed from the savagery of cannibalism. Their clothes were described as scanty and far from clean . . . . The other card, printed at a later date, had a much more dignified description of the Africans selling their lovely wares with their colorful native garb and exotic selves. I wanted to depict how someone was obviously enlightened

Suesan Stovall,
Jubilee. 2008.
Mixed Media

from the first printing to the last, and that the negative
wording was not "P.C."

In these days of war on two—or maybe more—fronts, and fatigue with politics growing chronic, Stovall's compilation covers territory too often over-
looked and rattles an all-too-often frozen attention span. Suesan Stovall's use
of earth shades and natural material connects, does not blink, and like an

aged and classic reworked leather-bound volume, screams and whispers to sinners and the righteous alike. The exhibition of thirty-seven pieces incites one to think, to look, and to hang on without preconceived expectations. This art does not show off, but crucial acclaim suggests that the artist will surely have a busy year ahead.

According to Henry Louis Gates, Jr.:

> Suesan Stovall combines the narrative brilliance of Jacob Lawrence with the mastery of collage by Romare Bearden, but with lyrical form. Her use of found objects is unprecedented in the African American artistic tradition. Stovall's work possesses and demonstrates an uncanny ability to capture the combination of history and passion.

Born and raised in New York City, Ms. Stovall, the daughter of legendary Peabody and Emmy award-winning journalist and correspondent Charlayne Hunter-Gault, attended the High School of Performing Arts, graduating with honors, before attending Sarah Lawrence College. Her vocal performances have brought her in contact with a host of bands, and she has performed around the world on soundtracks, and in music videos, theater, and film. Stovall's work has been exhibited in several other galleries, including the Schomburg Center for Research in Black Culture in New York City and the Tubman African American Museum, in Macon, Georgia. Ms. Stovall currently divides her time between Los Angeles and Martha's Vineyard. ⬡

Notes on Contributors

Moradewun Adejunmobi is Professor of African American and African Studies at the University of California, Davis. She previously taught at the University of Ibadan in Nigeria and the University of Botswana. email: madejunmobi@ucdavis.edu

Safoi Babana-Hampton is Assistant Professor of French at Michigan State University. She teaches twentieth- and twenty-first-century Francophone literatures and cultures. Her research interests include comparative and postcolonial Francophone studies. email: babanaha@msu.edu

Souleymane Bachir Diagne taught philosophy at Cheikh Anta Diop University in Dakar, Senegal, for twenty years before becoming a professor of Philosophy and of Religion at Northwestern University in 2002. He is currently a professor at Columbia University in the Departments of French and Philosophy. email: sd2456@columbia.edu

Rita Dove, Commonwealth Professor of English at the University of Virginia, is a former U.S. Poet Laureate (1993-1995) and the recipient of the 1987 Pulitzer Prize in poetry, among other honors. Her most recent poetry collections are *Sonata Mulattica* (2009), excerpted in this issue, and American Smooth (2004). email: rfd4b@virginia.edu

Petina Gappah is a Zimbabwean writer whose work has appeared in *The Times* (UK), *A Public Space*, *PEN America*, *Prospect*, the *Zimbabwe Times*, and the website of *Granta*. She holds law degrees from Cambridge, Graz University, and the University of Zimbabwe and works in Geneva as an international trade lawyer. email: anelegyforeasterly@gmail.com

Joseph E. Inikori is Professor of History at the University of Rochester. He is the author of *Africans and the Industrial Revolution in England: A Study in International Trade and Economic Development* (2002). email: jinikori@rochester.rr.com

Jeffery McNary has written several articles on U.S. politics and the arts, including a work on the poet Robert Pinsky, "The Amazing Mr. Pinsky." McNary's writing has been published in the *Rolling Stone*, *Newsweek*, the *New York Observer*, the *Vineyard Gazette*, and elsewhere. He is currently crafting a screenplay and divides his time between Cambridge, Massachusetts, and Paris, France. email: jeffmvy@netscape.net

Miranda Pyne is currently in a postgraduate program at the London School of Hygiene and Tropical Medicine. She is the recipient of an award by the Arts Council of England to complete her book manuscript, *From the Notebooks of Antioch Sy*. She lives in Boston. email: miripi_2000@yahoo.com

Rebecca Rosenberg worked as a freelance journalist in Cape Town, South Africa, before earning a master's degree from the Columbia University Graduate School of Journalism. Currently, she works as a freelance journalist in New York.

Ngũgĩ wa Thiong'o is is a novelist, essayist, playwright, journalist, editor, academic, and social activist from Kenya. He is currently Distinguished Professor of English and Comparative Literature and Director of the International Center for Writing and Translation at the University of California, Irvine. email: ngugi@uci.edu

Paul Tiyambe Zeleza is the Liberal Arts and Sciences Distinguished Professor and Head of the Department of African American Studies at the University of Illinois at Chicago, as well as the President of the African Studies Association. His publications include *The Study of Africa* (2007) and *African Universities in the Twenty-First Century* (2004). email: zeleza@uic.edu

Submissions

Send manuscripts to the Editors, Transition, *104 Mount Auburn Street 3R, Cambridge, MA 02138. Manuscripts should be typed and double spaced. Unsolicited manuscripts will be returned only if accompanied by a self-addressed, stamped envelope.*

Advertising/List Rental/Discounts

Send inquiries about advertising, list rentals, and discounts on bulk orders to jrnlsads@indiana.edu

Book Reviews

Send copies of books to be considered for review to Transition, *104 Mount Auburn Street 3R, Cambridge, MA 02138*

Indexing

Transition *is indexed/abstracted in Alternative Press Index, American Humanities Index, A Matter of Fact, Index to Black Periodicals, PAIS (Public Affairs Information Service) International, Periodica Islamica, Media Review Digest, Consumers Index, and Current Index to Journals in Education. Older issues are archived online by JSTOR (the Scholarly Journal Archive).*

Permissions

Requests to republish material from Transition *should be submitted electronically at http://iupress.indiana.edu/ rights, except for requests for educational reprinting, which should be submitted to the Copyright Clearance Center.*

Subscriptions

To subscribe, please visit the Transition *website at http://inscribe.iupress.org/ loi/trs. Subscription inquiries can be directed to iuporder@indiana.edu. Individuals: electronic $32.40; print & electronic $39.60; print $36.00. Institutions: electronic $90.00; print & electronic $140.00; print $100.00. Foreign first-class postage for combined print/ electronic and print editions: $24.00. Foreign air-mail postage for combined print/ electronic and print editions: $36.00.*

Back Issues

For information on single issues, please visit the Transition *website at http:// inscribe.iupress.org/loi/trs, send email to iuporder@indiana.edu, or call 1-800-842- 6796 (from within the U.S.) or 1-812- 855-8817 (from outside the U.S.)*

Postage

Periodicals postage paid at Boston, MA, and additional mailing offices. Postmaster: Send address changes to Customer Service Department, *Indiana University Press, 601 North Morton Street, Bloomington, IN, 47404*

World Wide Web

Visit the Transition *website at http://www.transitionmagazine.com*

GST No. R126496330

Transition (pISSN 0041-1191; eISSN 1527-8042) is published by Indiana University Press, 601 North Morton Street, Bloomington, IN 47404-3797 and is an official publication of the W. E. B. Du Bois Institute for African and African American Research at Harvard University.

The editorial office of Transition *is located at 104 Mount Auburn Street 3R, Cambridge, MA 02138. Phone 617-496-2845; fax 617-496-2877*

Send business correspondence to: Indiana University Press/Journals 601 North Morton Street Bloomington, IN 47404 Phone 800-842-6796/812-855-8817; fax 812-855-7931

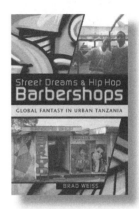
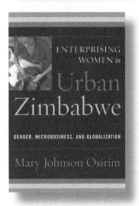